# Bucketmouth

*Fly-fishing for Trophy Bass*

*By Ken Morrow*

*ISBN 978-0-9885801-2-1*

# Table of Contents

# Introduction

Every trophy bass fishing expert will tell you that the most important thing you can do to increase your chances of catching a trophy bass is to fish in places that historically produce bass over ten pounds. If you want to catch them, you have to fish where they live.

All of those same experts will rattle off a list of the top five places where there is a concentration of fisheries with a demonstrated track record over a long period of time for producing trophy bass and their lists will all include Texas. But *East* Texas, in particular, has one distinct advantage that no other region can rival: Five of the nation's best-known "Big Bass Factories" lie within a three hour drive of each other!

As I write this, I'm sitting right in the heart of East Texas. It takes me less than an hour to get to Lake Fork, two hours to get to Sam Rayburn Lake, an hour and forty-five minutes to drive to Toledo Bend, and two hours and forty minutes to get to Lake Conroe.  For such a tight grouping of world-class bass fisheries, the games are really in East Texas and Florida.  But let's talk for a second about the best kept bass fishing secret of both Florida and East Texas, because everybody knows about the big name lakes.

Between the world renowned bass fishing lakes mentioned above - where consistent production of truly lunker size bass has attracted the world's tournament anglers, the TV cameras, and scads of bass fishing enthusiasts from all over the world - there are hundreds of smaller lakes and ponds that a) can't support and don't attract the crowds, and b) possess the exact same habitat qualities as the "big bass factories."  The plain truth is that I don't have to drive three hours in Florida or East Texas to catch trophy bass.  The landscapes are dotted will ponds, swamps, and small lakes (both public and private) that produce big bass just as well as the famous ones.  Realistically, you can drive about fifteen minutes in any direction from any one of these "bass factories" and come to another one just about as good at raising an impressive population of world-class bass! It's the real estate that matters: *the unique combination of the perfect year-round climate and perfect aquatic environments in which bass species can truly thrive to reach their genetic potential in their native range.* Just as it is in business, the three most important factors in improving your odds of success in trophy bass fishing are: location, location, location! *The first order of business is to put yourself where the big fish live.*

What far fewer people are aware of when it comes to East Texas is that within that same three hour driving distance, I have very realistic opportunities to catch Striped and Hybrid Bass from six to fifteen pounds on multiple fisheries. These opportunities are rare in Florida and geographically dispersed in California. About a fifteen minute drive from my house lies one of the best fisheries I know of for Hybrid Striped Bass. I've landed three over ten pounds in just over an hour from a kayak, with a fourth one breaking me off. On that same lake, an angler

recently landed a 13.22 lb. Largemouth Bass in a small

tournament. He was located no more than a mile from where I

caught those Hybrids. I also catch copious numbers of two to

four pound White Bass in this same lake. But you won't find

this lake on any of the lists of "best bass lakes in America." Why

not? Primarily because tournament pros are landing forty to

over a hundred pound stringers in televised tournaments on

Toledo Bend, Sam Rayburn, and Lake Fork. *Many terrific lakes*

*lie in the shadows of these legendary monster bass fisheries!*

In this book, we're going to talk about how to go about

consistently catching large bass in East Texas, but the same

principles and practices generally apply across the South. As fly-

fishermen, we have some unique capabilities and limitations

that affect our odds of catching world-class fish. Many of the

same strategies and tactics apply to conventional tackle and fly

tackle fishing for bass, but there are some differences.

Realistically, we are shallow water anglers. We also rely heavily upon a fish's ability to visually respond to our lures and we are more significantly impacted by strong winds and heavy chop. So we need to figure out specifically which fisheries in these densely packed "bass factories" offer our best opportunities for success.

Most fly-fishing literature focuses on the pursuit of trout in cold water streams. So the tackle, tactics, and techniques that produce the best results for bass fishing may be unfamiliar to the typical fly-fisherman who finds himself in East Texas. Bass behave differently than trout and salmon. So we'll need to learn what makes bass "tick." Many trout fishermen who find themselves casting into warm, still waters discover that it isn't hard to catch large numbers of small bass and bream, but they seem stumped when it comes to targeting large bass. That's because a bass's behavior patterns change once he or she grows to between twelve and fifteen inches. At that point, the fish no longer respond well to small flies that imitate tiny minnows and aquatic insects within three feet of the surface.

So the typical fly angler tries to satisfy himself with copious numbers of relatively small fish. Most will trade in their five or six weight trout rod for a two, three, or four weight. This book is about teaching fly-fishermen to catch the *big* fish we all know haunt these waters. The truth is that very few bass are beyond the reach of fly-fishermen, and I'm going to teach you how to do it.

# Chapter One

## Choosing Fly-Friendly Fisheries

East Texas has one of the highest concentrations of top tier tournament bass lakes in the world. Bass fishing is not just big business, it's huge business in East Texas! From just North of Houston to Texarkana, from just East of Dallas to the Louisiana state line, there are seven world renowned bass tournament fisheries and about a half dozen more second tier tournament lakes. Lake Conroe, Sam Rayburn Lake, Toledo Bend Reservoir, Lake Texoma, and Lake Fork are the biggest names. Lake Bob Sandlin, Lake of the Pines, Lake Palestine, Cedar Creek Lake, Lake Tawakoni, and Lake Ray Hubbard are the second tier angling destinations. All of these lakes have excellent infrastructure for handling large numbers of lake users at the same time. They all boast an active tournament schedule. You can hop from one to another with no more than an hour's drive between them, and often quite a bit less. All of these lakes are man-made impoundments. The only natural, non oxbow, public water lake in the state of Texas is Caddo Lake, which lies along the Texas-Louisiana border northwest of Shreveport. It is also a major bass fishing destination, but doesn't boast the full tournament calendars of the man-made reservoirs. Two more major bass fishing lakes in East Texas worthy of mentioning in this general category are Martin Creek Lake and Lake Monticello. This is because they are power plant cooling lakes impounded from swamp land, and they become very popular during the coldest part of the short East Texas Winter, mostly January and February, when water temperatures in the big lakes hover in the fifties and dip into the upper forties. Due to the power plants' hot water discharges, these two lakes maintain a year-round water temperature that never drops below the mid-seventies, which is ideal water temperature for Largemouth Bass.

These are the lakes that everyone knows about and visits. But these lakes comprise only a small portion of the impounded surface water in East Texas. Almost every town in East Texas has a lake named for the community. These are generally medium sized and small lakes ranging from a few hundred surface acres to about five thousand surface acres. Additionally, there are hundreds of smaller lakes, both public and private. Scattered between all of these lakes (more than 100 acres of surface area), there are scores of ponds (less than 100 acres flooded). Some are municipal ponds. Some are on public land owned by the state. Many are on private property. In short, you don't have to drive much more than a mile or two anywhere in East Texas to find a

Sealy Big Bass Splash weigh-in on Sam Rayburn Lake in Deep East Texas. These amateur tournaments draw crowds of thousands and are major social events in the communities in which they occur. Sealy's Big Bass Splash is the oldest continuously operating bass tournament series in the United States.

bass fishery. You may have to get permission from a private owner to access some of them, but they're here. What's more, about ninety-five percent of them have the potential to sustain very large bass. Almost every fishery accessible to the public in this part of Texas is managed for Largemouth Bass fishing, to some extent or another. This same situation is replicated in Florida, Georgia, and...to a lesser extent...Alabama and Louisiana.

Texas has a very good fisheries management program for private landowners, too. There is a large and sophisticated network of members-only bass fishing clubs that leases access rights to intensively managed private lakes and ponds in East Texas. But for every pond or lake in their inventory, there are at least ten more private lakes or ponds with healthy, sustainable bass populations that are not enrolled. I could spend the rest of my life fishing a different lake or pond in East Texas that is available for the asking and barely scratch the surface.

East Texas also has a number of rivers and creeks that provide excellent bass fishing opportunities. The Sabine, Neches, Cypress, and Trinity Rivers are the four major watersheds in the region. The Red River forms the northern boundary of East Texas. These rivers flow from and through a number of the larger impoundments. Then there are White Oak Creek, Lake Fork Creek, Big and Little Sandy Creeks, and the Sulphur River...just to name a few of the best tributaries within these watersheds. From Lake Conroe southward to the Gulf of Mexico, there are a number of bayous and canals that also contain good opportunities to catch big bass. In recent years, there has been a renaissance in small boat infrastructure for navigating these courses in the form of the Texas Paddling Trails.

How do we choose the ones that are most likely to provide the best possibilities for fly-fishermen to catch trophy bass from this vast array of fisheries? *We will look for a few key factors that all exist in the same body of water.* Then we will *avoid* the fisheries that do not meet all of these criteria and focus our fishing activity on the ones that possess them all. These criteria will change a bit, depending on the species of bass we're fishing for. And lakes have different characteristics than streams do. So I've divided this topic down into the following categories: Black Bass Lakes, Temperate Bass Lakes (Hybrids, Striped Bass, and White Bass), and Bass Streams. The goal is to find the fisheries that will provide the best fly-fishing opportunities to catch Largemouth Bass over twenty inches (or four pounds and up), Hybrid Bass over twenty-five inches (over seven pounds), and White Bass over sixteen inches (which will range from just under two pounds to just over four pounds).

## For Traveling Anglers

If you don't live in East Texas, but want to spend several days to several months fishing here for trophy bass, there is good news. East Texas has a very low cost of living and an ample supply of short-term rental accommodations. Ranging from campgrounds to lake houses with private boat docks, renting a place to stay in East Texas is a bargain. Predominantly rural, the lifestyle here is relaxed. Groceries, gasoline, utilities, and the full range of entertainment options are economically priced. Almost every large lake has multiple choices for RV and tent camping, and many are full-scale waterfront camping resorts. There will also be a number of homes available for short-term rental on and near the water. Some are large, updated homes in gated communities that would be unaffordable in most other places in the country. Some are mobile homes that rent for a few hundred dollars per month. Boat, RV, and mini-storage facilities dot the landscape. Every little lake has at least one restaurant near the water, and many of them are surprising values for the price. Bigger lakes have multiple vendors competing for business. True to our rural roots, we have a full schedule of festivals, farmers markets, swap meets, and parades to distract you from fishing. Canton's First Monday Trade Days is the world's largest swap meet, and runs for three days preceding the first Monday of every month. Antique shopping is big business in East Texas, too. We have one of the best rural healthcare infrastructures in the country. We have plenty of fishing tackle stores and bait shops, both large and small, and there is no shortage of boat and trailer dealerships and repair shops.

If you've never been to East Texas, don't expect the typical Southwestern high desert landscape that everyone imagines from the movies. Geographically, East Texas has far more in common with Louisiana than it does with the majority of Texas. The land is heavily forested with ample surface water. Here in East Texas, "seafood" staples include fried catfish and boiled crayfish. The region produces a lot of beef and very little pork. We also produce a large portion of the nation's chicken. The Tex-Mex and traditional Mexican restaurants here are very good and very affordable. It's far more "Old South" with a Lone Star Republic twist than most people imagine it would be. I've always been surprised by the number of West Texans who come to East Texas every Spring and Summer just to hang out with our trees. Forestry and nursery businesses are a huge portion

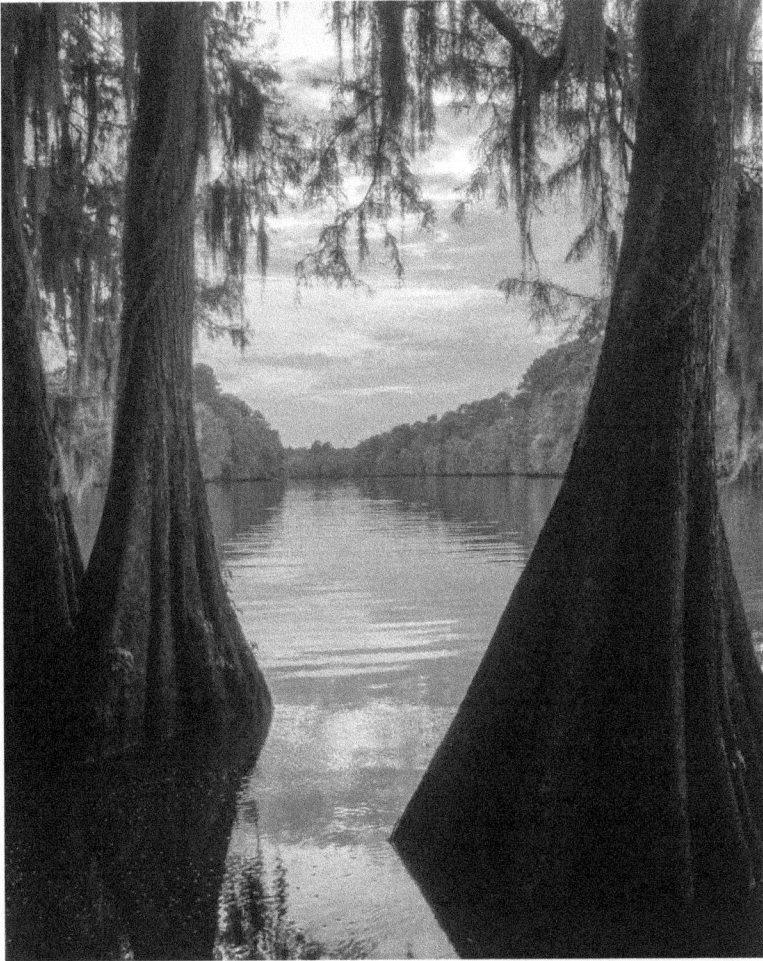

Caddo Lake State Park. (Earl Nottingham, Texas Parks and Wildlife Department)

of our agricultural landscape, and we produce a significant portion of the nation's peaches, blueberries, roses, and ornamental shrubbery. The people are predominantly polite and hospitable. People on country back roads still waive when they pass one another. Complete strangers still hold doors for one another, even when no one is carrying anything in their arms. Adult strangers still refer to one another as "sir" and "ma'am." All things considered, East Texas is a very "fisherman-friendly" place to visit.

## *Best Black Bass Lakes in East Texas*

Now we turn our attention to selecting the lakes in East Texas that will provide fly anglers with the very best chances of catching trophy sized Largemouth Bass (aka Black Bass). As we've previously discussed, most of the lakes in East Texas of any size will have all of the basic ingredients for growing and sustaining populations of big Largemouth Bass. They'll be chock full of Gizzard and/or Threadfin Shad, Fathead Minnows, Bluegill Sunfish, Crayfish, leeches, frogs, Hellgrammites, Damselflies,

Dragon Flies, aquatic worms, Salamanders, grasshoppers, water snakes, and small rodents (along shorelines). That's the Largemouth Bass's menu. Water temperatures will range from the low fifties to the mid-eighties, depending on the season. Dissolved oxygen levels are generally very good. Since most of the lakes are impounded wetlands, creeks, and rivers that we refer to as "dish pan lakes" due to their relatively shallow depths and gently sloping shorelines, there is an abundance of structure and cover. Periodic droughts, combined with municipal and industrial water use, cause fluctuating water levels in many of them; helping to rejuvenate aquatic vegetation in shallow water areas and along shorelines. Most are actively stocked and managed by Texas Parks and Wildlife Department (TPWD).

It is what makes them *different* that we are interested in. There are four things that I am looking for when I'm selecting good lakes for Largemouth Bass fishing in East Texas:

1. Low Turbidity – in other words, *clear water*.  I am looking

for water that the fish can see well in.  Fly-fishing is heavily

Largemouth Bass in clear water.

dependent upon fish being able to find your lure with their eyes. Due to the need to keep our offerings extremely light-weight, we have to forego most of the spinners, buzzers, rattles, and lips that cause conventional lures to create a lot of ruckus in the water. Fly-fishermen rely primarily on visual cues to entice fish to strike. So I want to fish water where the fish can see pretty well.

2. Protected Water – fly angling is more adversely impacted by high wind than bait or spin-casting fishing methods. As a fly-fisherman, it's not practical to drop a couple of lines off the stern on down-riggers and start trolling when the wind gets up too high to cast and the chop on the water gets sporty. We have to cast to our fish, and our casting is adversely impacted by the wind more easily than with other rod and reel methods. So I'm looking for forested banks, undulating terrain, and lots of natural and man-made features along the shoreline to break up and/or provide cover from winds in excess of about fifteen miles per hour. If you've ever been out on the wide open

portion of a big Texas lake, you know that the chop, current, and wind gusts can be just as bad as they are when fishing the coast. Since I cannot control the wind, I want to find places where I can get out of the brunt of it and keep fishing. *Primarily, I'm looking for an abundance of small coves and long peninsulas surrounded by hills and mature trees.*

3. Fish Density – I research fisheries using lake records by species and Texas Parks and Wildlife Department (TPWD) survey data. TPWD tracks lake records separately for fly-anglers and reports all tackle records. Don't let that fool you and cause you to misinterpret the data! Just because the fly tackle lake record for Largemouth Bass on a particular lake is only three pounds, it does not mean that the lake doesn't hold a bumper crop of fish over four pounds. There aren't many fly-fishermen in East Texas, and few of us submit records. Fewer still of us fish water more than about six feet deep or with heavy tackle and big flies sufficient for enticing and landing big bass. These realities tend to skew the fly rod records for many lakes downward. The main

thing we're looking for is the presence of big bass! I don't care how they are caught or if they're shocked up in a survey. But I will look at the fly rod records, because it will give me some sort of hint about what my shallow water opportunities might be. For example, several lakes that I fish have all tackle state records over ten pounds and a fly rod record under four pounds. I've caught numerous fish over eight pounds from all of them. So I have come to interpret a lake record over twelve pounds and a fly rod record close to or over four pounds as "high potential" for catching large bass on a fly. One of the best ways to get a sense of what size bass are being caught in a lake is the Texas ShareLunker Program, which allows anglers to track in near real time via the Internet where truly large Largemouth Bass are being caught. When anglers catch a Largemouth over thirteen pounds, they are rewarded for turning it over in healthy condition to TPWD, where it used for a selective breeding program. When you see a lake producing a high percentage of these fish, you can infer two things. First, there are a lot of big fish in that lake. Second, there are a lot of people fishing that lake.  For us, that's both good and bad news, as you'll see below.

4. Relatively Low Boat Traffic – *Less boat traffic directly correlates to water clarity in East Texas lakes, but it also correlates to lower fishing pressure.*  A lot of folks think that it is purely a function of water temperature that drives big bass deep in East Texas lakes, but I believe that's only *part* of the story.  Boat traffic explodes exponentially on most of the big lakes in East Texas from March until November...when the weather is warm.  As temperatures rise, more Texans take to the lakes.  This is especially true on *weekends and between Memorial Day and Labor Day weekends*.  All of that boat traffic and fishing pressure causes fish to seek shelter.  Deep water is safe water for large fish.  They're getting away from the cacophony of sound waves and vibrations in the water caused by churning props, racing engines, and slapping hulls.  The most popular lakes in East Texas are often popular because they have reputations for consistently producing huge bass.  But the

hordes that descend upon them on weekends to chase that dream put all of the fish down. So I want relative peace and quiet. A nervous fish isn't eating *anything!*

This doesn't mean that I won't fish Lake Fork, Sam Rayburn, Toledo Bend, or Conroe. It means that I *rarely*...usually under protest...fish them on weekends. These lakes are huge. There are "backwater" areas of these lakes that are beyond the main traffic patterns. If I'm going to fish one of these "tourist lakes," that's where you'll find me. There are just as many big ole bass hanging out in the vast majority of the lakes in East Texas - same fish, but less competition. Calm fish instead of nervous fish. Sounds like better odds to me!

I've already mentioned the correlation between boat traffic and turbidity. A bunch of boats out there tooling around for half a day will churn up any shallow lake. This phenomenon is obvious anywhere that the water is often gin-clear in its natural state. It can be crystal clear all week long. Then the weekend brings about ten times more boats, and by noon the water that was clear this morning is now brown. For every action there is an equal and opposite reaction. The displacement of water caused by boat hulls and propellers is *cumulative*. And in a lake, it has nowhere to escape. This stirs up the loose layers of silt on the bottom. As these particles become suspended in the water, visibility and light penetration are reduced. Things are harder for the fish to see. In fact, excessive turbidity has been proven to stunt the growth of Largemouth Bass by making it harder for them to find food.

The commotion in the water caused from all that boat traffic not only drives the fish deep, it also provides an auditory and visual camouflage for the bait on which they feed, making it harder for the predatory fish to distinguish the sound waves and vibrations from each other. It's a classic "white noise" scenario. When you have trouble understanding what someone is saying in a place with a lot of background noise, you're experiencing the same thing. Fish that can't see or hear are nervous, and nervous fish don't eat unless they're extremely hungry. That doesn't mean that the total absence of other people is going to make it easier for you. In a serene, natural environment where you are the only alien predator, you stick out like a sore thumb. Such situations, often highly prized by skilled anglers, actually require a high degree of stealth and very subtle and life-like presentations. One "foreign" sound, shadow, or movement can put fish down, because their senses are totally uncompromised. What we're really looking for is a balance that tips the scales in our favor. I never shy away from fishing pressured waters. I avoid *busy* waters because...as a general rule...*so do the big fish*.

Basically, this means that we're going to de-emphasize those "bucket list" lakes. We may fish their out-of-the-way places, mostly in less popular times. Otherwise, we're going to focus on second tier and off-the-beaten-path lakes where everything else we're looking for lines up and leave the "big name" lakes to the bait and spin-casting fishermen, pleasure boaters, and skiers. There is one exception: the West half of Lake Fork. Due to an abundance of exceptional habitat in relatively isolated coves and the population density of huge Largemouth Bass, the fly-fishing for trophy bass here is excellent most of the year.  But I do try to avoid it on weekends.

*The existence of springs within a lake or pond is a key to finding high water clarity (low turbidity).*  Spring-fed impounded wetlands are abundant in the central portion of Northeast Texas that lies between I-20 and I-30 from Lake Fork and Van Zandt County to the Louisiana border.  The turbidity of these lakes is not so heavily influenced by rain events as it is in most East Texas lakes.  They tend to stay clearer most of the time, and water clarity returns more quickly after heavy runoff.  One of the best examples I know of is the pond inside Tyler State Park. This spring-fed sixty-five acre pond is exceptionally clear and has a very good population of Largemouth Bass in the four to eight pound range.  It's well sheltered by the surrounding forest and rolling hills.

Lakes that are bordered by and downstream of new housing and commercial development, new oil and gas operations, and row-crop agriculture will see higher turbidity rates than lakes downstream from and adjacent to well established vegetation and few parking lots. Poultry farming operations, particularly the presence of Consolidated Animal Feeding Operations (CAFO's) can result in higher than desirable nutrient loading in lakes, which increases algae blooms. Algae blooms increase turbidity and deplete dissolved oxygen as they begin to die. Keep these things in mind when scouring maps in search of clean water.

Lake Holbrook and Lake Hawkins in Wood County, West and East of Mineola, respectively, are medium size lakes fed by both creeks and springs with good water clarity and plenty of shallow water habitat. The first twenty inch bass I ever caught in Texas came out of Lake Holbrook in 1980. My largest Largemouth Bass caught on a fly was a twelve pound, twenty-six inch brute caught on a Wool Head Muddler Minnow at Lake Hawkins. I know of two more excellent bass lakes between these two, but they're both privately owned. One requires that you be a resident of the sub-division that surrounds the entire lake to fish there. That's Lake Brenda in Mineola, which is primarily an excellent White Bass and Redear Sunfish fishery. The other is a Largemouth Bass lake between Highway 80 and the Sabine River just East of Mineola. It is a high-end private fishing club property named Woodvale Lake. But there are numerous private ponds and lakes surrounding Mineola and Hawkins that produce astoundingly large Largemouth Bass in very respectable numbers. This is some of Texas' best surface water resources, and the water table is very shallow. That's why they call the area I just described "The Lake Country."

A bit to the North, you'll find Lakes Quitman and Winnsboro, just outside of the Wood County towns of the same name. Other lakes of similar profile are Lake Lydia, Mineola Club Lake, the lakes at Holly Lake Ranch, Lake Gilmer, and many private lakes on ranches scattered throughout Wood County. One of the best big ponds open to public fishing in all of East Texas lies on the outskirts of Canton. It's perfect for fishing from a kayak or canoe. It lies on city property and routinely produces four to six pound Largemouth Bass year-round. This is a soil conservation district impoundment known as Canton City Lake.

Another great mid-sized lake that is a state park with a solid reputation for producing trophy Largemouth Bass is Purtis Creek State Park, East of Mabank near Eustace, Texas. At almost three hundred fifty acres, Purtis Creek Lake fishes best in the hottest part of summer, which is unusual. I believe that is due to the boat restrictions on this lake. Check them out before you plan a trip. Water clarity is better than average for East Texas lakes. The all tackle record on this small, off-the-beaten-path, public lake is 13.73 lbs, 27" Largemouth Bass (all tackle). The fly rod record is a 5 ½ pound Largemouth caught by Clifford Hilbert on a popper in early November, 2004. Lake Athens is another of those municipal lakes that is less than 2,000 acres, and boasts excellent Largemouth Bass fishing. The lake record is an 11.36 lbs, 29" Largemouth caught in 2003. Don't overlook the state park lakes. In my opinion, they provide some of the best fly-fishing for Bass and bream in the country; an opinion that is shared by the Texas Parks and Wildlife Department's Regional Director of Freshwater Fisheries for East Texas, Mr. Craig Bonds:

> "Smaller, state park waters can offer the perfect combination of factors mentioned above. Places such as Purtis Creek, Daingerfield, Tyler, and Lake Raven inside Huntsville State Park are great small waters, offering excellent fly-fishing opportunities."

Among the larger lakes that rank pretty well on my list for Largemouth Bass, there are a few to the North and East of Wood County worth mentioning. Lake Cypress Springs, Lake Bob Sandlin, and Monticello Lake are directly adjacent to one another southwest of Mount Pleasant. Lake Monticello's popularity increases as temperatures drop in other fisheries, because it is a power plant cooling lake. It is one of Texas' most popular Largemouth Bass fishing lakes, but its "hey day" was decades ago. The fourteen pound, twenty-nine inch lake record

Largemouth is impressive, but that fish was caught way back in 1980. The lake still produces a lot of trophy quality Largemouth Bass, and at 2,000 acres of water that never dips below seventy degrees, it's pleasant to fish all year. Watch for dense fog on cold mornings.

Cypress Springs has the cleanest water of the three lakes in this chain. It's heavily spring-fed and surrounded by forest. It's half again bigger than Monticello. The two are separated by Bob Sandlin. Cypress Springs Lake is the furthest upstream on Cypress Creek, which is a tributary of the Cypress River. The lake record is a 13.69 lbs Largemouth caught back in the 1990's. Bob Sandlin is the biggest of these three lakes at about nine thousand acres, and is home to another nice State Park. It is much deeper than the other two lakes in this chain on Cypress Creek, reaching depths of sixty-five feet. The record Largemouth from Bob Sandlin is the biggest of the three at about fourteen and a third pounds, caught back in 1990. But recent surveys and fishing reports indicate that the best may still lie ahead for this lake. However, it isn't the most conducive to catching big bass *on the fly rod*, as evidenced by the 3 lbs fly rod record. When you combine this information with the average depth in the lake, you get the first clue that you aren't going to reach many of the big fish in this lake with a fly. Visiting the lake or inspecting topographical maps, you'll see that the land around the lake is steep, with rolling hills and bluffs bracketing the valley which has been turned into the lake. It's a pretty lake, but pressure is on the way up, clarity is not as good as in Cypress Springs, and there isn't a lot of shallow water habitat. These things make the lake harder to access big bass with a fly rod, but it can be pretty good for White Bass and even Crappie on the fly.

In the 2014 Freshwater *Fishing Forecast* edition of the *Texas Parks and Wildlife Magazine*, the East Texas District Fisheries Biologist, Richard Ott, cited three lakes he found to be holding particular promise. At the time of publication, the entire state was still in the throes of a multi-year drought, and lake levels were suffering tremendously.  This impacts fishing pretty

severely because boat ramps can become high and dry,

rendering them useless, and because shallow water habitat for

bass and forage fish is the first to dry up as water levels drop.

But many of the smaller, off the beaten track, lakes in East

Texas are very drought-resistant.  And Richard focused on three

of them:

> Lakes Lone Star, Monticello, and Gilmer should
>
> maintain their water levels and offer consistent
>
> largemouth bass, sunfish, and crappie fishing.
>
> Gilmer produced a Texas ShareLunker in 2011.
>
> (*Hooked! Texas Fishing 2014.* Texas Parks and
>
> Wildlife Magazine, Austin, Texas. Pg. 32)

This is just a sampling of the lakes that are pretty much "top

of mind" to folks familiar with the portion of East Texas that lies

north of the Sabine River, often referred to as Northeast Texas.

This is by no means all of them!  Further east, you'll find Caddo

Lake, which is mostly a big old-growth hardwood timbered

swamp. It is Texas' only natural inland lake that is open to the public. There are a few large ponds and/or small lakes that are entirely privately owned, as well as some natural oxbow lakes along the rivers. Historically, it has been great fishing for many species of fish and a duck hunting paradise. In recent years, Caddo Lake has suffered from the proliferation of an exotic aquatic weed species that has just about choked the life out of much of the lake. When vegetation gets this dense, access becomes problematic, game fish have trouble finding enough forage to achieve maximum growth rates, the amount of sunlight is reduced, and various chemical properties in the water can change in ways that are detrimental to the survival and growth of Largemouth Bass. The vegetation is so thick in much of the lake nowadays that you cannot get a boat through it. In the past year, TPWD has reported promising progress in fighting the weeds, but the real work is just beginning.

Lake Palestine is a large lake that lies just west and southwest of Tyler, Texas. For much of the year, a lot of the lake is turbid enough that fly-fishing becomes more challenging, except when fishing top-water flies. But there are portions of the lake where water clarity is good, especially during Winter. I tend to fish bulkier and darker flies for Largemouth and Hybrids in this lake. Unfortunately for Largemouth Bass fishermen, the average water temperature in the Winter in most of the big lakes in East Texas is dipping into the upper forties and peaking in the low fifties. That makes fishing for Largemouth Bass a little tough, because they become very lethargic. However, Lake Palestine is excellent from Fall through Spring for big Hybrid Bass and White Bass. We'll talk more about that later.

We could keep moving south and continue this from now until the cows come home, but I think I've made my point. The big lakes further to the South that everyone knows about are Sam Rayburn and Toledo Bend. This is the region we refer to as "Deep East Texas." I have not fished Toledo Bend for Largemouth on a fly rod, but I would like to do so up in the northern end where it is shallower and has a lot of timber and smaller coves, in the stretch where the Sabine River becomes Toledo Bend Reservoir. I have fished Sam Rayburn enough to know that the best fly-fishing opportunities for Largemouth are also in the upper portion of the lake. Sam Rayburn is an impoundment on the Angelina River, and the upstream portion of the big arm of the lake is the part locals call "up in the timber." It's basically a flooded hardwood swamp. In the Spring, during the bass spawning season, it gets hammered. You see, Sam Rayburn, Toledo Bend, and Fork are all three lakes where you have no chance of winning a bass fishing tournament without catching at least one ten pound Largemouth Bass per day. That reputation draws a lot of Bass fishermen when those bruisers come shallow to spawn! I like to fish these lakes early and late in the spawning season, but I try to avoid them in the middle. I'll tell you why.

Largemouth Bass don't have calendars or watches, nor do they give a rip what the gal at the gas station, or fisheries biologist, or the marina owner said. They spawn when they feel like it.  So they don't all spawn at the same time.  You'll generally find plenty of pre-spawn and post-spawn bass when folks are saying "it's on right now!"  That means some bass haven't spawned yet and others are already finished.  One can only logically conclude that some fish spawn early and some fish spawn late.  So there will be a fairly constant stream of big Largemouth Bass making their way to the shallow breeding grounds for quite a bit longer of a stretch of time than what is typically considered "the spawn," and I have come to believe that the "peak" of the spawn is not really all that statistically significant with regard to your odds of catching a big Largemouth on the fly.  *You better get out there and fish whenever you can during this time of year.  It typically begins at the end of February and lasts until early June in East Texas.*  For me, I know I should be fishing for Largemouth and White Bass when I see Dogwoods blooming.  That's when it begins.  It is directly related to the angle of sunlight penetrating the water. It is *not* directly caused by water temperature, like most people believe.  However, it does correlate to water temperature, because the angle of sunlight and duration of days has a huge impact on water temperature. So we generally say that once the water warms back up into the sixties, the party is on. Once the Sun tells the fish it's time to reproduce, various factors impact their actual decision to do so: water temperature, water quality, weather patterns, the fish's health, and so on. But they all begin to "stage," or move toward the shallower water and hang out there based on the angle of sunlight and length of days. If it happens to be cooler than usual or warmer than usual, that won't substantially change the start and stop dates of the mating ritual, but it may very well alter the peak spawning periods. So this is when your big fish are on the move, in need of more energy, more aggressive than usual, *and actively searching for stuff to eat.*

Once the females get on the beds, they aren't interested in food. They'll strike to defend their nest, but they aren't worried about food until after they make babies. We'll talk more about these things in detail later on in the book, too. For now, just remember: when the Dogwoods bloom, it's time to be fishing as much as possible. That won't end until it turns consistently hot and muggy. Today is June 5th, and it just turned hot and muggy on May 30th. Each year is a bit different, but not by much. I won't bother with the top tier tournament lakes except on weekdays during this time frame. But I don't care whether I catch an eight or a fifteen pound Largemouth Bass. If I catch a ten pounder, I've caught a fish that few anglers ever will. And the availability of ten pound Largemouth is pretty good in scores of lakes and some ponds all over the region. What makes those lakes famous is the remote possibility of a fourteen pound bass. So I feel no need to go to the same place everyone else is going. Like Sam Walton always said, when I see everyone turning right at the intersection, I'm going to turn left. In all my life of hunting and fishing, that has never steered me wrong. But that's because I do my homework and find out where *else* my quarry is located. You can't just ignore conventional wisdom and fish in a mud puddle. There has to be a good reason for your destination. But following crowds increases the competition, risks, and hassles. It's true in business, and it's true in hunting and fishing. I actually learned that lesson as a young teenager from a Whitetail Deer expert from Stephen F. Austin State University...and a few big bucks. Years later, I read it in Sam Walton's biography.

So where is "Left?" That's the big question, isn't it? If I told you specifically, it wouldn't be "Left" anymore. Would it? But I'll make this as clear as possible. I spend eighty percent of my fishing time during peak bass fishing season on lakes that I have already mentioned, that are not famous tourist destinations, that do not host televised big-money bass tournaments, and that are open to the public. These lakes are generally far smaller than the famous lakes. They are typically much clearer than the big lakes. Only two of them have water more than thirty feet deep, and you'll never find me near that deep water. You'll find me in less than fifteen feet of water, usually less than ten. They range in size from less than a hundred acres to about three thousand acres. I don't have to drive more than an hour to get to any of them from my house.  This Winter and Spring, I have landed at least one bass over twenty-five inches about half the times I've been out fishing.  Fishing with a fly rod, I have not been skunked in over a year...and I only get skunked in saltwater.  I have gone fishless for a day of fishing in fresh water three times in my entire life that I can recall.  The big lakes that I actually fish for trophy bass with any frequency are Lake Fork (for Largemouth) and Lake Palestine (for Whites and Hybrids).

## *Best East Texas Lakes for Hybrids & White Bass*

Now we'll turn our attention to identifying trophy waters for Striped, Hybrid, and White Bass in East Texas.  What makes a lake great for Largemouth Bass is similar, but not the same, as what makes them great for temperate bass.  For starters, temperate bass are most active when the water is colder.  They become more active as sunlight decreases.  So fishing for them is best very early in the morning and late in the evening, as well as on cloudy and rainy days.  They are not very sensitive to turbidity. Their diet is a bit more selective than the Largemouth Bass's diet, too. They live almost entirely on shad. They'll eat Fathead Minnows if they have to, but not if there are shad to be eaten. When we talk about "trophy" size Stripers in this part of the country, we're talking about a fish over ten pounds. That's barely a Striped Bass in some parts of the world not too far from here. When we call a Hybrid a "trophy fish," we're generally talking about a fish that is over twenty four inches, and will tip the scales at least to seven pounds. Hybrids don't get much bigger than about fifteen pounds. They're very impressive runners and fighters when they're in the seven pound class! Pound for pound, they're probably the "hottest" fresh water fish I've ever caught.

So the first thing we're going to look at is the lakes with good populations of shad, particularly the Threadfin shad. Don't get me wrong: temperate bass will eat plenty of Gizzard Shad. But Threadfin do not generally grow as large as Gizzard Shad, which can grow as big as White Bass do. A big Striper or

Hybrid will devour a pretty good size Gizzard Shad, but White Bass are out of the hunt when the shad get more than about four inches long. Furthermore, the smaller shad (both species) are very susceptible to cold water. They become disoriented, lethargic, and even die when the water temperatures dip into the forties. They start looking for warmer water and more cover in the low fifties. For a small fish like this, water that is too shallow for the big temperate bass is a safe haven, and it also warms up more quickly during the day. So shad will crowd into slightly deeper holes in shallow water by the thousands to keep warm. When this happens, the Temperate Bass follow the large schools of shad as far into the shallows as they can. For White Bass, this means a foot of water or so. For the much larger Stripers and Hybrid Bass, I rarely find them in less than five feet of water. White Bass seem to prefer to congregate in the deeper pools in shallow water, where the water is three to ten feet deep. They'll wait here for migrating shad and bust them ferociously. You'll find these conditions occurring in the Fall, Winter, and early Spring in the shallow creek and river mouths that feed into the big lakes. In early Spring, the spawning run begins in the same parts of the lake tributaries, concentrating the temperate bass populations.

You see, Temperate Bass are relatively pelagic fish, meaning they prefer deep, open water versus orienting closely to structure. It also means they tend to suspend at various depths, whereas over three fourths of Largemouth Bass are within a foot of the bottom at all times. They school more readily than adult Largemouth Bass do. So they are most plentiful in larger lakes, especially Stripers and Hybrid Bass. White Bass do quite well in some lakes as small as a hundred acres. When their food supply starts to congregate in shallow water, so do they. This can be in shallow coves, on windswept flats off of points, and in the mouths of rivers and creeks. Generally speaking, the larger the body of water, the bigger the bass will be. And there will be more of them. But it all depends on that healthy, thriving population of shad.

Now you're going to actually key on the big lakes, including the ones with the big reputations. Lake Fork, Lake Texoma, Lake Palestine, Lake Tawakoni, and Toledo Bend are all fantastic fisheries for temperate bass. Texoma is the best game in the region for Striped Bass. On Lake Texoma, the Stripers come shallow and feed hard on schools of shad from sometime in February or March until well into the early part of Summer. On Lake Fork and Lake Palestine, you can fish to large schools of shallow White Bass year-round in the early morning and just before sunset. But the prime time during which they will remain active throughout the day runs from sometime in February until sometime in May. On Lake Palestine, the Hybrid Bass run big and mean. It's a great winter fishery for conventional tackle guys, but you have to pick your battles to catch them on a fly. There will be days from November until June where you can find them in water less than fifteen feet deep. Hybrids tend to take a bit more after their Largemouth cousins with regard to orienting to structure and ambushing their prey. But they'll orient to major structure along choke

49

points in the migration routes of the shad to lay in wait in deeper holes than White Bass typically do in the same situations. They also chase big schools of shad in deep, open water. But I catch most of mine in about ten feet of water. So you're looking for big lakes with an abundance of underwater road beds, bridges, culverts, and other permanent structures that were flooded when the lake was created. Above-water bridges are good places to look, too. The bigger the lake, the more of that sort of stuff there usually is. Lake Palestine is an excellent example. White Bass make good spawning runs up the river and major creek mouths above these lakes in March and April. Don't be dissuaded by murky water when chasing temperate bass during the spawning runs. They like a bit of current. So they'll become very active during run-off periods following heavy rain. Just as predictably, White Bass schools will herd and bust big schools of small shad in shallower, more protected coves nearly every morning and evening of the Spring and early Summer. They will also do this on huge humps or submerged islands and shallow road beds that are just a few feet underwater. Sometimes you find these in surprising places far from the bank in wide open water. The water may be more than ten feet deep, but you can easily catch these fish on a weighted fly and floating line or with a sinking line and weightless fly when fishing it in the top four feet of the water column. Sometimes, when things are just right for the first hour or so after daybreak, you can catch them on top-water flies – sliders, poppers, and such that imitate wounded shad. And if things get really still just after sunset but before dark, the same thing can happen.

Those are my favorite lakes for catching really big Stripers, Hybrids, and White Bass with one exception. The little spring-fed lakes of the Lake Country almost all have a good population of White Bass. The action can be fast and the fish often grow to trophy sizes, which for White Bass is anything from three to five pounds. These fish will be fifteen to twenty inches long.

On the big lakes, one of the best ways to locate feeding Stripers or Hybrids is to look for concentrations of shorebirds,

Cormorants, ducks, hawks, and eagles. These birds will congregate on big schools of shallow shad, and so do these game fish. If the birds are there, the Stripers and Hybrids are probably there too. Since we don't troll as fly anglers, finding the birds is your best bet. Conventional anglers tend to troll and look for birds at the same time. Sometimes they find the fish before they find the birds. As fly-fishermen, we don't have that option. Scouting the birds on big lakes really requires a fairly quick motor boat.

Another great lake for White Bass is Toledo Bend, but we're going to talk about it in the section about streams for one particular reason.

## Choosing Bass Streams in East Texas

If you really want to experience a great White Bass spawning run in East Texas, you cannot miss the stretch of the Sabine River just above Toledo Bend Reservoir. From the spot where the river meets the lake upstream for at least a dozen miles, the Sabine River hosts one of the most spectacular White

Bass runs in the world each year in March and April. It may

begin in late February. It might not begin until the middle of

Professional guide, Carey Thorn, with a pair of trophy White

Bass. (Image: Carey Thorn, 2012.)

March.  It will continue for about a month from when it begins.
Take a canoe, kayak, or small river skiff of some sort.  You move
from hole to hole below the riffles and catch White Bass until
your arm hurts.  You can do this daily while the run lasts.  There
are a couple of campground outfitters that run guide services
for this stuff and you can camp and access the river right from
their waterfront properties.  RVs and tents are both fine.  The
weather is excellent that time of year for tent camping,
notwithstanding the inevitable rains.  March and April are too of
the wettest months in a typical year in East Texas.  But it
doesn't rain every day.  Furthermore, rain improves the White
Bass fishing!  They are oblivious to muddy water due to run-off,
like a bit of current for spawning, and never seem to lose their
appetite.  It seems to me that the worse White Bass can see, the
more aggressively they attack lures and flies near the surface.
They bite best when it's dark, cloudy, or raining.

26/03/2007

Russ Doughty is a good friend of mine with a nice White Bass he

caught while we fished a creek together in 2007.  We caught a

stringer full that were all about this size.

Another great run of large White Bass (bigger on average than on the Sabine) is the Neches River above Lake Palestine. This only goes on for a few miles of river from the top of the lake upstream north of Highway 31. The run is typically shorter, lasting only a couple of weeks most years. I have known it to go on for a month, but at a less frenzied pace – as if the spawn was staggered. That can happen when unusual weather events interrupt the run, like a serious cold snap or a major rain event. This year, we had both and the spawning run was longer and slower than usual.

The Kickapoo Creek arm of Lake Palestine also gets a pretty good White Bass run, but I've always found higher numbers of big fish on the Neches River.

Other than that, I'm not a big fan of river or creek fly-fishing in East Texas. There are some great bayous and canals in the far southern part of East Texas, beginning South of Lake Conroe and just North of Houston, where you can catch some nice

Largemouth Bass.  But I try to stay as far away from Houston as possible, and rarely venture as far South as Lake Conroe.

I do know that the Crappie fishing can be pretty good on the Trinity River from the town of Trinity down to Lake Livingston. The lake is known as a pretty good White Bass lake.  So I would imagine that the White Bass run would occur up the Trinity River just a bit ahead of the others, and is probably pretty good. But I have never heard about or experienced it.  That's a pretty stretch of river for float trips, and the largest river in East Texas by water volume and width from bank to bank except for the Red River, which forms the border between Texas and Oklahoma.  A quick look at the TPWD website suggests that there is a good White Bass run up the river and tributary creeks, but it is nowhere near as famous as the one on the Sabine River above Toledo Bend.

Now we know *which* lakes, ponds, and streams to fish for the best chances of catching truly trophy size bass on the fly in East Texas.  These principles will largely translate to anyplace in the Southeastern USA with some minor tweaking. Since there is some seasonality to when various lakes are most likely to produce the best shots at different species of trophy bass, you're going to want to focus on different lakes at different times of the year. I suggest you select no more than three fisheries to begin with. Learn to fish each one until you're consistently catching trophy bass before seeking out new ones. You'll pursue Largemouth Bass in the Spring and early Summer, then switch to temperate bass in the Fall and Winter. You may want to toss in some Spring trips for White Bass during their spawning runs, and remember that Hybrids and Striped Bass also follow these migrations. They just don't run so far up in to shallow water. You'll find them in the river and creek arms of the lake in about ten feet of water instead of way up in the rivers and creeks in a few feet of water more often than not. You can also choose a power plant lake for Fall and Winter Largemouth Bass fishing if you want to focus solely on those strains of bass.

Jeff Poole with a 31 pound Striped Bass he caught on a 6 weight

fly rod using a TNT Fire Tiger articulated streamer in July, 2014.

In the next chapter, we'll learn more precisely where to fish within those lakes, ponds, and streams on which we have chosen to concentrate, and on when to fish for them.

# Chapter Two

*The Genius of Subtraction*

Now that you've chosen two or three fisheries on which to focus your fishing for trophy bass, you'll want to fish these lakes or streams as much as possible and resist the common urge to sample unfamiliar waters until you are consistently catching trophy sized bass on these two or three fisheries. True genius is the art of subtraction. Learn to eliminate the non-essential and focus on what is essential. Learn to play to your strengths and avoid the traps of your weaknesses. So you are going to want to pick fisheries that meet your needs and are most convenient for you to fish. This will help you fish them more often. If it is expensive and requires overnight trips to fish them, your budget and schedule will force you to fish them less frequently. I choose fisheries that are no more than an hour's drive from my house to focus on for trophy fishing. This way, I can fish whenever I have at least four hours available. Fishing more days *and fewer hours per day* will also improve your odds of scoring big with more frequency than if you fish long hours over fewer days. You'll soon learn why this is true.

The next thing you'll need to do to narrow your focus is to figure out which areas and what types of habitat on each lake are most likely to produce trophy sized bass consistently. Bass do move around, but Largemouth Bass don't move very far from where they're born. Most Largemouth spend their entire lives within a mile of their birthplace. Their preferences will change with the conditions. But most lakes in East Texas have a lot more in common than they boast of features that make them unique. Remember, we're trying to find big bass in ten feet of water or less so that we can reach them with flies. If necessary, we can get down to about fifteen feet with specialized equipment. Beyond that, there's not much use in fly-fishing for them. So where are we going to find bass in shallow water?

Most people know that trophy sized Largemouth Bass tend to come shallow and hang out in less than fifteen feet of water in this region between the beginning of March and the end of May. This is pretty reliable. But you will find Largemouth Bass in very shallow water with less frequency all year long. You just have to know where to look for them and do so often. When I asked Craig Bonds, the Regional Director of Freshwater Fisheries for TPWD, to boil it down to brass tacks, this is what he said:

> Big bass need four things: food, shelter from direct sunlight, favorable water temperature and dissolved oxygen, and security (*from predation and harassment*). If all four of these factors exist in shallow water, big bass will be there. Shallow water anglers should be looking for the presence of prey fishes like sunfishes, minnows, shad, and crayfish; and cover like boat docks, timber, rocks and aquatic vegetation. Without these, bigger bass will move deeper and further offshore.

Largemouth Bass predictably hang out in water we can fish effectively with fly tackle in the following situations:

1. Near the banks.  Most of the clues we're looking for will be along the shoreline.

2. Overhanging trees.  One of my favorite shoreline structures to fish is where there are big trees right on the bank.  Old trees, especially hardwoods, are critter-magnets.  They provide food and shelter to a wide variety of fauna.  Mice, snakes, lizards, and frogs...all big bass food...gravitate to mature trees.  They will use deadfall to scurry or slither out for a drink of water, to catch their own food (mostly insects), and so forth.  Now and then, they'll fall in the water.  Sometimes, big bass will knock them into the water in order to make a quick meal of them.  The shade provided by large trees also provides additional concealment and cooler water for the bass.  Cooler water holds more dissolved oxygen, which big fish need to survive.

3. Emergent vegetation.  Areas where plants have their roots in the water and then grow to the surface (and beyond) make great places to fish for large bass.  All the smaller stuff

Overhanging trees along the shoreline creating shaded water.

Emergent vegetation along shore line.

they feed upon use this habitat as cover from predators. Like a maze, the foliage below the surface creates a bunch of ways to hide, evade, and escape. Many of these plants are also sources of nutrition for the things these smaller fish, reptiles, and rodents feed upon. The plants also produce oxygen as a by-product of photosynthesis. This increases the dissolved oxygen level of the water. The exceptions to this are certain algae blooms and decaying vegetation, which reduce dissolved oxygen. If you see mostly brown vegetation mass floating on the surface, that's a good indicator that big fish won't be there (except during the winter when most plants are dormant). Lily Pads are a favorite of mine, because they encourage frogs and mice to hop along their massive leaves supported by strong stems out over the water where bass can lie in wait beneath. Bass will notice the vibrations of the leaves caused by the pitter-patter of tiny feet or a slithering snake. They will track the movement from below and wait for whatever is making this racket to slip into the water. Sometimes, huge bass will explode on the moving pads in an effort to knock their prey into the water. I once caught a very big Largemouth Bass with a deer hair frog that was resting on top of a Lily Pad. During the retrieve, it popped up onto the pad. I paused for a second to scratch my nose or adjust my glasses and BAM – the whole Lily Pad disappeared in a splashy swirl. I set the hook without much hope of success, and I came away firmly connected to one of the bigger Largemouth Bass I've ever caught. Don't drop your guard! Stay ready. Dense Lily Pad beds will create a nearly solid canopy over one to four feet of water (sometimes a bit deeper). Shade from overhead cover is a huge key to the likely presence of big Largemouth Bass. I never skip Lily Pads when fishing for them. There are some other types of aquatic plants that form rafts of stems and leaves at the surface, particularly along banks. Bass will often hide out under these to avoid direct sunlight.

4. Docks and other man-made structures over the water. Shade from the sun and shelter from avian predators are both things that big bass seek. Largemouth in particular, like to lie in

the shallow water under docks, boat houses, etc. They will almost always be tucked well back into the structure, and not out past the edges in open water. Now and then, you may find one out there. It's rare, but it happens. They're at the docks for shelter and shade. They will ambush an easy meal, but won't move far without significant coaxing. Casting must be accurate. Tight loops cast overhead, off shoulder, and side-arm become critical to success. This is where a great repertoire of roll casts is really handy. Your casts should be long and retrieves short. One of the advantages of fly-fishing is the ability to pick the fly up and re-cast as soon as your fly is outside the "strike zone." This allows fly anglers to back off from a target, make accurate casts from further away, work the fly only in the "hot zone," and then pick it up and re-cast. Bait and spin casters cannot do this. To fish this cover efficiently, they move in close, cast, and retrieve their lures all the way to the boat before casting again. Most of that retrieve isn't very productive and they risk putting the fish down by getting closer to minimize wasted time and effort.

Boat houses and docks create protection from sun and predators. Combined with a tree-lined bank that is casting shade over the surrounding area, this is prime Largemouth Bass habitat.

5. Bridges, culverts, and road beds. These structures also provide cover and concealment, but they also tend to channel the bass's prey into smaller spaces. The water over submerged road beds warms up faster and stays warm longer than surrounding water, and provides an excellent opportunity for shallower bass when water temperatures are cooler in the Fall and Winter, early in the morning, and during the night. Submerged and emergent culverts hold the same attraction, and sometimes allow the only narrow choke-point through which aquatic creatures can pass from a ditch or pond into a larger body of water, between two ponds, etc. Large Bass will lay in ambush alongside the openings. Focus on the shady side of submerged linear structure when water temperatures are in the sixties or warmer. I recently tested this with a student of mine. We both paddled our kayaks out to a long ruined bridge that is right at the surface of the water crossing a submerged creek early on a summer morning. I had him fish the shady side while I fished the sunny side. We used the same flies and techniques. He caught several nice fish, and I caught none.

6. Retaining walls. Retaining walls will either provide warmth or shadows...sometimes both. If bass need the warmth, they'll stick close to them. If there is a good amount of bait holding there, a big bass may lie in the darkest shadow and wait for an easy meal.

7. Flooded timber. When the lakes fill up, the trees go underwater – either partially or entirely. They usually die either way, but some trees will survive for many years of constant root submersion. We refer to this as "green timber." The dead stuff is "ghost" or dead timber. Stumps are the remnants of fallen dead timber. All of this stuff holds bass. The bad news is that the big fish stick very close to the timber. You'll have to learn to bump stumps if you want to have success. The occasional fish might chase your fly away from a tree in clear water, but not often. The bass also tend to hold on timber no shallower than about half way between the bottom and the surface of the water. Quite often, they're near the bottom and hugging a tree. I've never had much luck fishing surface flies or lures in flooded

Lily Pads in flooded green timber. Big Largemouth Bass live here! (Bob Laminack, 2014.)

timber, although I know a few buzz-bait specialists who catch their largest fish this way. I don't like to fish flooded timber without snagless flies or in more than about six feet of water. Let me explain why not.

I fish for bass with about a four to seven foot leader. If I am in six feet of water, bouncing a fly along the bottom, and I get snagged up and cannot get the fly loose, I can get right on top of the fly, reach down in the water with my scissors or knife, and cut the leader instead of the fly line. If I'm in ten feet of water when that happens, I'll be lucky to be able to reach down below the fly line and cut the leader. That will cost me a fly line, leader, and fly instead of a leader and fly. My fly lines cost between seventy and a hundred dollars each. A fly costs me pennies to make myself and leader costs me a couple of bucks. If you're doing this type of fishing right, you're very likely to get hung up pretty well now and then. The same thing is true if a big bass wraps you up on a log underwater. I can reach down about two and a half feet or so from a boat, but not much more. And I don't want to cut fly lines.

8. Creek mouths.  Not right in the creek mouth, but adjacent to them, there is often a lot of emergent vegetation and/or overhanging trees.  These are great places for big bass to ambush their food from relative seclusion.  They're also usually adjacent to some deeper water for a quick escape, even if it's only the creek channel itself.  *I catch a lot of my biggest Largemouth Bass in or along the edge of emergent vegetation in the mouths of creeks in the backs of coves.*  This is what I mean by the genius of subtraction.  I find docks and emergent vegetation along a shady bank with over-hanging trees in the very back end of a huge cove with a small feeder creek emptying into the lake and I focus on that small area, ignoring the rest of the cove.

9. Submerged grass beds.  Just off the bank of most East Texas lakes, there is a grass line.  The weed bed will be several feet to several yards wide with two edges.  The edge

The back of a protected cove where a feeder creek dumps in to an East Texas lake. The banks are lined with ten feet of emergent vegetation for almost a hundred yards beyond the mouth of the creek. The open water is studded with flooded dead timber in four to ten feet of water. Early morning and late evening bring a lot of shade to this area, and I've caught many huge Largemouth Bass here.

closest to the bank is called the *shallow edge*. The edge furthest from the bank is the *deep edge*. Big apex predator bass *rarely* hang on the shallow edge of a grass line. They almost always cruise along the *deep edge*. You can catch a lot of smaller bass and plenty of pan fish by fishing the inside edge of a grass line throughout most of the year, but if you want to catch the big boys, you need to focus on the *deep edge*. In the hottest part of Summer, nearly all fish will be associated to the *deep edge*. The water is usually several feet deeper on the deep edge than it is on the shallow edge. This is usually not a sight-casting area. You are fishing the area blindly. We'll talk more about this later in the book, but you have to choose between a lot of small fish that you can sight-fish to in a couple of feet of water versus trophy bass in three to ten feet of water. This book is about how to do the latter.

10. Shallow coves. If an entire cove doesn't get much more than fifteen feet deep, then you're in a good area for fishing for

Dead timber studding a shallow cove in a large lake in East Texas.

bass with a fly!  Now find the spots where other features listed above occur in the cove.  Focus on those areas.

Temperate bass often herd large schools of shad into coves like this and then feast on them out in open water.  If you see fish popping the surface out in the middle of a shallow cove, that's what you're watching happen.  When this is big Hybrids or Stripers, it will be extremely evident.  They will cut bulging wakes, make huge splashes, and turn massive boils.  If it's just popping (with expanding rings on calm water), then it's likely to be White bass.

11.  Submerged "islands."  By definition, this is a very large hump surrounded by deeper water where the bottom rises to no more than about three feet underwater and remains that way for at least a quarter of an acre or so to several acres of surface area.  It is not unusual to find schools of bait fish and a few big bass on a hump like this.  Most frequently, you'll find the bigger bass on the edges of these humps, not in the middle of the shallow area.

12. Points. Off of every peninsula on a lake or in a river (land surrounded by water on three sides), you will find a shallow area that continues the slope of the land far out into the water. This often creates rather large areas of shallow water directly on line with the peninsula. Sometimes, they hook to the left or right. Small to medium sized bass love this type of water, and they'll cruise around whacking minnows in such places. Truly big Largemouth are rarely found in this type of habitat unless you just get lucky and catch one passing through. But Stripers, Hybrids, and White Bass love this kind of water! This is particularly true when the wind is blowing against the point, because this will push minnows and small shad into the shallow water. The wind-driven water becomes very turbulent when it hits the shallows, and shad become disoriented. This is a smorgasbord for temperate bass.

13. Leeward shorelines. On windy days, big Largemouth tend to move to the protected shore. They're following the

bait.  Temperate bass will often favor the windward shore, as I noted above.

14.  Sunny banks in the morning and shady banks in the evening.  The sun warms the water.  During the cool season, Largemouth are going to "warm up" in the morning by moving into direct sunlight.  When it gets too warm, they'll look for shade or a deep hole to cool off.  In the afternoon, it's been warming all day.  Fish tend to move into the larger shady areas along the shore...or even to the shady side of a submerged island, road bed, etc.

15.  Submerged buildings, creek beds, ponds, and fences. All of these types of underwater structure provide different habitat features that bass find attractive.  If they're shallow enough to reach them with a fly, you might want to check them out.

16.  Deep Holes below shoals.  This is for the creek and river anglers who are hunting for White Bass.  For big White Bass,

you want to focus your attention in the deep holes right where a creek or river begins to turn into a lake. Sometimes, this type of bottom feature may continue for several miles upstream. Start at the downstream end of this type of habitat and work your way upstream until you find the fish. Focus on holes that are two to three times deeper than the main stream bed. The bigger the better, but don't overlook the smaller holes entirely.

Focusing on parts of each of your trophy bass fisheries where you find the highest concentration of these types of fish-holding features will significantly increase your odds. So eliminate all parts of the lake where none or only one of these features exists. Ignore those parts of the lake or stream. Subtract them from the equation. Narrow your focus and invest your time and effort where it can be most productive.

By now, you're probably thinking, "I'm going to need detailed maps of these lakes." You're right. So this might require you to add something instead of subtracting it. My personal recommendation is that you learn to use Navionics on a computer, tablet, or your cell phone.  If you have a sonar GPS plotter on your boat, hopefully it is Navionics compatible.  If not, it would be worth it for you to upgrade.  Bar none, these are the best full-featured navigation and fishing maps in the world.  But you will quickly find that the interactive features included in Navionics software is a true game-changer.  Fly-fishermen really don't need sonar for about two thirds of the year, but the GPS-enabled charts are invaluable.  Get the highest resolution nautical maps of each of your trophy fisheries that you can find.  Study them.  The mobile apps you want are called Navionics Boating, and you'll definitely want the Navionics+ upgrade for it.  The Navionics website has an interactive global mapping feature that will work on your Mac or PC.  And the software package you want for your GPS chart plotter on the boat is called Navionics+.  I don't recommend many specific products in this book, but Navionics is one of the few that is so demonstrably superior to anything else on the market that I believe the brand and model actually make a major difference.

By studying these maps, you can quickly hone in on the areas in your fisheries where you have the highest concentration of the features you're looking for – the features that hold big bass – in the best combinations. These are the locations you're going to fish.

For example, if you find a shallow cove with a submerged creek bed that has a couple of submerged road beds and old flooded bridges across the creek, this is a good area. If that same cove has a bunch of grass beds with emergent vegetation and flooded timber in it, that's even better. And if the cove is oriented so that the surrounding trees provide shady and sunny shorelines that alternate as the day progresses, that's awesome. If the trees are thick and tall enough to provide significant shelter from prevailing winds, you just hit the jackpot! But this is just one example of the possible combinations that indicate prime lunker bass territory. The more habitat feature density you find in the smallest possible space, the better off you are. You will hunker down on these parts of the lake and focus your trophy fishing activity in such places, while forsaking the remainder of the lake, enabling you to spend much more time with a fly in front of fish than traveling around from place to place. Chances are that no matter what fishery you choose, it will have multiple high-probability locations. When you move from one to another, don't dally. There may be plenty of fish to be caught along the route from Hot Spot A to Hot Spot B, but we're hunting for trophy bass. Fish the places that hold larger numbers of smaller fish with your grand kids.

Just as we have used a process of subtraction to determine where to fish, we're also going to apply this to the age-old question: when to fish. But don't forget: once you're fishing where the fish are, the next most important element of success in trophy fishing is how much time you spend with a fly in the water. Just as the most successful duck hunters and deer hunters are the guys who spend the most hours in the blind, the most successful trophy angler is going to be the person who kept a fly in front of fish the most. *So the first rule is: go fishing whenever you can.*  With that said, there are days of the week and hours of the day that are more productive than others.  Some are not so obvious to most fishermen.  Then there is the time of year when your odds are best.

We've already discussed when the peak seasons are for catching trophy Largemouth Bass and temperate bass, and they do overlap:

Largemouth Bass – from the time in March when the Dogwood trees begin to bloom until sometime in June is *peak season*, but you can catch trophy Largemouth on the fly most of the year in most lakes and in the dead of winter in the power plant cooling lakes.

Temperate Bass – the *peak season* for catching them is during their upstream spawning runs and in the dead of winter when the shad kills occur.  Roughly, this is from sometime in November until sometime in April.  But there is some excellent temperate bass fishing on some fisheries in East Texas well into the summer. You simply have to find the bass whacking shallow schools of shad early in the morning and late in the evening. This usually happens on the windward side of points and well back into shallow tributary coves in open water.

During these peak times of year, fish as much as possible. But some days and some time frames are still better than others. So, depending on your flexibility of schedule, you'll want to keep these notions in mind:

1. The vast majority of fishermen believe that the fishing is best from the crack of dawn until mid-morning. Most plan their fishing activity around this notion. That means most serious fishermen are on the water from the crack of dawn until mid-morning. Many stay out until mid-afternoon. Few at all fish from dinner time until dark. Likewise, you will generally see other boaters and skiers on the water from mid-morning until about dinner time. The boat ramps tend to get busy with people exiting the water sometime between three and five

o'clock. And that's when the wise trophy angler goes fishing on weekends!

2. The vast majority of boaters still have jobs. Boats cost money. You have to earn it to spend it. So the number of boats on the water will almost invariably spike exponentially on weekends and holidays. If you can fish on weekdays, do so as often as possible. If you fish on weekends and holidays, focus on the time from mid-afternoon until dark. If you can't fish in the evening, fish from dawn until mid-morning. From July through September, the first couple hours of daylight and the last couple hours before dark are by far the most productive times to fish for bass. Once things cool off significantly in November and lasting until the Dogwoods bloom in early Spring, early morning is not actually the best time to catch trophy bass. During this time of year, I catch nearly all of my bass in the afternoon and evening. I figured this out when I was thirteen years old and have become more convinced of this reality over the thirty five years that have followed.

A lot of bass fishermen will tell you I'm nuts, but I have found that boat traffic plays a major role in the success or failure of bass fishing and in-shore saltwater fishing. All that commotion makes trophy fish wary and nervous, pushing them to deeper water. Most bass fishermen can learn to fish deep and overcome this problem to some extent, but fly anglers simply don't have that option. When I realized that I was catching virtually all of my trophy bass on the fly in the late afternoon and evening, I all but quit fishing in the mornings. I rarely fish on weekends. My typical trip to the lake begins in mid-afternoon and I have a fly in the water before four o'clock. Then I fish until dusk. The only exception is July through September, when I prefer to fish from the crack of dawn until about ten o'clock. If I'm fishing for trophy bass, it is very rare indeed that I don't catch at least one that is at least twenty inches long. About half the time, I'll catch at least one over twenty-five inches long. Those are trophy bass. And I've lost count of the number of bass I've caught over ten pounds on a fly rod. Just this season, I've landed four that were more than ten pounds on the fly, and it is the beginning of June as I write this. I average about a day of true trophy fishing per week. Trust me, if you follow this formula for a year, you won't go back to fishing with the crowds.

If you cannot fish on weekdays, don't despair. On weekends, fish in the early morning and late evening when recreational boaters and skiers are uncommon. The point is to do whatever you can to avoid the busiest times on the water. Don't follow the crowds if you can avoid it. If you can't avoid it, just realize that the game has changed. Your odds of catching a trophy bass on a fly are lower, but that doesn't mean it won't happen for you.

So the genius of subtraction is to reduce the equation to only the places and times that are most likely to yield the desired results, and to concentrate your best efforts and as much time as possible in those places and times. It really does just come down to pure math, but probability includes randomness. There is always variation and you might just get lucky. That's what keeps life interesting. Learn to view the tasks of targeting and timing as a process of elimination. Simplify. Get rid of all that is unnecessary, and especially that which is counter-productive. This will keep you from becoming distracted by that proverbial "the grass is always greener on the other side of the fence" impulse. Know what you're doing and why. Then work your plan. As a fly casting instructor, I spend an amazing amount of time eliminating counter-productive and unnecessary motion from my students' casting strokes, mends, and retrieves. I have noticed the same phenomenon when teaching knot and fly tying. I'll stop someone and ask them, "Why do you do that?" Most of the time, they ask, "Do what?" They don't even realize they are doing it. I'll explain and demonstrate what I am asking about, and most can't provide me with a reason for the extra steps they've incorporated into their efforts. Many times, they had no idea they were even doing it. But trying to get them to stop doing it can be daunting, because they've done it so much that it has become a habit. *The secret to true mastery of a task is to simplify it down to the essential, eliminate everything else, and then perfect the*

*essential elements to the best of your ability.*

27.5" Largemouth Bass caught on a size 2 Wool Head Muddler

in 2014 from a spot I've already shown you in this book.

# Chapter Three

You're going to need a boat. Sorry, but there's no way around it. If you want a decent chance at catching a trophy bass, you'll need to transit to your fishing spots via the water. Most of your best fishing spots will be inaccessible from the bank. Even though some of the creeks and rivers may be practical to wade and fish in some places, you'll want to transit from shoal to shoal over miles of stream. Furthermore, almost all land in East Texas is privately owned. This is no less true along the streams. If a stream in not on the list of navigable waterways of the state, then the landowners have the right to deny trespass via water. In other words, you can't even float a boat down it without their permission. That will certainly force you to get permission to wade in it. Get a boat.

"Boat" is a very broad and non-descriptive term for anything that is designed to carry passengers or cargo to transit the water. You're going to want a boat that is appropriate to the task of catching big bass while fly-fishing. That rules the vast majority of boats out. We don't want submarines or aircraft carriers. Sailboats are probably not a good choice. You want a small fishing boat no longer than about twenty feet that will not obstruct your ability to cast. No roofs, no cabins, no overhead ski rails. So rule out the runabouts and cabin cruisers. Avoid any pontoon boat with a permanent roof. With those gone, there are still thousands of choices in boats that are readily available. Here are some key features you're going to find very useful.

The most important quality I look for in choosing a boat is buoyancy. I like boats that float. That might sound pretty self-evident, but a lot of today's most popular small fishing boats are not very buoyant. Let me explain.

The U.S. Coast Guard has a standard for USCG approved watercraft. Most kayaks and canoes do not meet this standard. Some jon boats don't meet this standard. Many skiffs don't meet this standard. And there is only one drift boat that I know of (a row boat made specifically for swift rivers) that meets this standard. *The standard is that a boat must be able to continue to float when the main deck and cockpit are filled with water.* In other words, if the boat is swamped, it still floats. It will not sink. This requires integrated flotation modules added to the hull. Most kayaks and canoes have none of this. Some jon boats have none or too little. That's because internal flotation adds weight. If I'm going to be in water that is too deep for me to stand up in, I want a boat that will float even if it fills with water. I strongly advise you to do the same. Another option that dramatically improves the buoyancy...or seaworthiness...of a boat is a self-bailing hull. In other words, the boat will quickly drain any water that comes over the gunwales, bow, or stern. In my opinion, I simply must have one or the other, and preferably both, for any boat I plan to take in water more than about five feet deep. This is just a simple matter of dramatically improving my odds of survival in an emergency.

The next thing I want in a boat is a smooth deck and gunwales that will not create unnecessary problems with fly line while fishing. Bow-mounted trolling motors, as well as most electronics modules, rod holders, and other accessory systems mounted on the boat will all snag slack fly line. I keep this stuff to the bare minimum of what I must have to operate safely and efficiently. Bimini tops can be great for taking breaks or staying out of a brief rain shower, but they must fold down completely out of the way on the stern of the boat.

The third thing I really look at closely when choosing boats is their comfort. If a boat is uncomfortable to operate for long periods of time, then it's not going to be much fun and I'm not going to spend that much time in it. Comfortable seating is a must! This is critical with jon boats, canoes, and kayaks.

Next, I want a boat that moves and sits quietly on the water. I don't want a lot of hull slap in the little wind-driven chop on a lake. I don't want the boat to creak or squeak or make other noises when I move around inside of it. A double hull boat will transmit less noise into the water when I pick things up and set them down inside the boat. There are no radios on my fishing boats except for the emergency radio.

I'm also a bit particular about hull colors. Bright, shiny boats are beautiful, but that's more appropriate for a pleasure craft than a fishing boat. I want my boats to blend into the surroundings as much as possible. They're going to cast a big shadow into the water below anyway. Adding glare and contrast to the mix above the surface is an unnecessary hurdle for me to overcome. I don't want the fish to realize I'm there. There is a flip-side to this discussion, though. *From a safety standpoint, it is much better if your boat is as visible to other human beings as possible.* You'll have to decide what is right for you. When I'm fishing saltwater, I like boats that are very light colored, but preferably with a matte finish that reflects less glare. The water is generally very clear, fish most often see it against the backdrop of the sky, and the bottom and shoreline are often sandy. In a bass boat, I want a neutral earth tone color like tan, brown, gray, or olive.  Color probably isn't a deal

killer, but when buying a boat you have a choice.  Why waste it?

The color that turns black first when viewed through water is

red.  Blue and purple transmit very well through water.

Finally, I want a boat with a high weight capacity and plenty

of room for anglers and gear.  I'm not a big fan of sophisticated

storage solutions, rod holders, and unnecessary features in a

fishing boat.  But I do want to be able to keep my gear

organized and out of the way of navigation and fishing activities.

Beyond these fundamentals of what makes a decent fly-

fishing boat, there are a million things to argue about and fret

over.  The biggest choice you're going to make is whether or not

you want a motor.  When it comes to bass fishing, that's the

biggest denominator between fishing boats.  You'll either rely

upon paddles, peddles, or an outboard motor.  That will

determine the types of boats you choose to look at.  Paddle and

peddle craft allow for a much higher degree of stealth, the

ability to operate in very shallow water in tight spaces and thick aquatic vegetation, and provide the operator with healthy exercise. Motor boats increase your range, tolerance for rougher water, and load capacities at the cost of stealth, ease of maintenance, and safe operating depth. Frankly, I'd prefer to have one of each.

I have found motor boats very useful for bass fishing in lakes in East Texas from twenty-four foot pontoon boats to fourteen foot jon boats, with all of those sixteen to eighteen foot bass boats in between. Pontoon boats draft amazingly shallow for their size and cannot be operated at high speed. They're very safe and comfortable. If they have no permanent roof structure over the cockpit, they are easy enough to fly-fish from. Trolling motor mounts can be installed well away from the main deck area so that they don't snag fly line. The deck is not in contact with the water and the pontoons and deck on a well-built model have sound dampening features, making them very quiet. Personally, I think pontoon boats don't get as much credit as they deserve as excellent fishing boats. I've caught some nice bass off of them over the years.

Bass boats are fine craft for bass fishing, but I find that a lot of people who pay top dollar for the fancy ones are afraid to put them in the kinds of places where the really big Largemouth Bass live. That's ironic and sad. If you can't afford an occasional prop or trolling motor repair, then you cannot afford a thirty thousand dollar boat. Trolling motor mounts on the bow of bass boats are problematic for fly-fishing. This can be mitigated by tossing a wet towel over the trolling motor mount and control wires, but it's still there and still gets in the way now and then.

A jon boat with a small gas motor or even a big transom-mount trolling motor work pretty well for bass fishing on East Texas lakes, except when it comes to competitive fishing or the need to outrun a sudden severe thunderstorm. Some minor modifications to most jon boats can make them much more "fly-fishing friendly." From the factory, they come with some problems with regard to fly lines.

Something similar and far superior to a jon boat is the new Shallow Water 16 skiff from Hog Island Boatworks. This boat's modular accessory system paired with an excellent roto-molded polymer skiff hull and internal flotation really set this boat apart. You can add up to about a forty horse outboard, but probably would never need more than 25 hp. These boats draft two inches of water without passengers and gear with a thirty horsepower motor mounted on the stern. They draft about four inches with a couple of two hundred pound fishermen on board. But they will handle chop, wind, and wakes much better than the typical jon boat. They are U.S. Coast Guard certified as "unsinkable."

A close second is a Carolina-style skiff or a Boston Whaler of the same basic class. These are excellent, seaworthy, quiet, shallow draft motor boats that don't require too much motor. They're comparably inexpensive. These boats (at least in the

Hog Island Shallow Water 16 (SW 16) at work on the lake.

name brand versions) come with internal flotation and self-bailing hulls.  So they are also U.S. Coast Guard certified.

Another relatively inexpensive option that is quite popular because it is so effective is the Bass Cat type of rigid polymer catamaran-design pontoon boat.  These are generally between six and twelve feet long with one or two swiveling pedestal seats.  They're typically powered by a trolling motor.  I've fished from several over the years, and they're quite safe and effective.

For me, the ideal length of a skiff, bass boat, or jon boat for the lakes in East Texas is between sixteen and eighteen feet.  When you get any longer, some places you want to hunt bass get too tight for safe operating.  Any smaller and the transits across the large expanses of open water become extremely sporty at times, reducing the boats to torture chambers instead of pleasure craft.

Personally, I do most of my lunker bass hunting with a fly rod from a paddle craft. I prefer the aesthetics, exercise, stealth, and maneuverability of kayaks and canoes when I'm serious about catching big bass on East Texas lakes. Many of my biggest bass are caught in places that motor boats simply cannot go. Well, maybe they could go, but they're likely not to return. Many of the places I target consist of entire coves covered in aquatic vegetation like Lily Pads with intermittent flooded timber and shallow spots that are less than a foot deep. There aren't many motor boats that can operate in the thick stuff. But I can paddle my kayak right through it without any difficulty, especially by standing in the boat and paddling with a stand-up paddle.

After many decades on the constant quest for the perfect paddle craft for this kind of work, I finally found a boat that I don't think could be improved upon. Nowadays, I fish from a Nucanoe Frontier 12. This is a twelve foot long wide bodied hybrid kayak that is part canoe, part pirogue, and part kayak.

Fishing partner, Trey Parker of Palestine, Texas, working some

Lily Pads from his Nucanoe Frontier 12.

I've upgraded the seat to their Max 360 seat on a Rigid seat base and use the optional stand-up rail and Transformer Paddle. It's the ultimate combination of functionality, comfort, and safety as far as I'm concerned. It's a simple boat to operate. The only sophisticated thing about the boat is the intelligence of the design. But I still plan to add a motor boat in the future. Currently, I'm leaning heavily in favor of the Hog Island SW 16, but I may just end up buying an 18 to 20 foot pontoon boat for its added safety, comfort, and capacity. After all, a big part of the value in a motor boat is the ability to comfortably and safely fish with more people on board. Most bass boats and skiffs are only good for two anglers. A pontoon boat in that size range can safely fish up to four anglers in the right configuration. They're also a superior fishing and pleasure boating platform for small children and people with disabilities, and that's important to me.

# Chapter Four

We're all familiar with the old proverb, "A poor craftsman always blames his tools." I've seen plenty of credible examples in media over the years of the little boy who caught a record book fish on a Snoopy pole rigged with a bobber and a hook baited with Velveeta cheese. I've even witnessed some pretty amazing catches of trophy class fish on tackle not suited to the purpose. Yes, it happens. It is very rare. That's what makes these stories noteworthy. In no way is this evidence that someone can successfully target and land trophy fish on dime store children's tackle designed for a trip or two to a park pond to catch Bluegills. But there is more than enough high-quality, affordable fly tackle out there that will help you catch more big bass. So don't get hung up on brand names, marketing hype, or status symbols. Acquire appropriate gear that you can afford.

The reason why there is so much diversity in the fly tackle market is primarily due to specialization. I've known a couple of golfers who only carried a driver, a nine iron, and a putter to play 18 holes of golf when the conventional wisdom is that you need a whole bag full of woods, irons, wedges, and putters.  It is possible to make those three clubs suffice for almost every shot in golf.  But these guys were excellent golfers who reduced their club selection as a combination of two desired goals.  First, they wanted to reduce the weight they lugged around the course.  They walked for the exercise, but were old men who didn't want to lug a forty pound bag full of clubs and other paraphernalia around the course in the summer heat every day.  Secondly, the enjoyed the added challenge.

The purpose of this book is to teach you how to improve your odds of catching large bass on a fly, not to make it more challenging.  Having the best possible tackle for the task will definitely improve your odds of success.  That doesn't mean you have to spend a fortune.  Frankly, there is a lot of hyper-inflated pricing based on hyperbolic marketing claims in the fishing tackle business, and the fly-fishing tackle sector has it in spades! Pay attention and I'll save you hundreds to thousands of dollars.

*There is absolutely no practical reason on God's green Earth to spend more than five hundred dollars on a fly rod, or more than about three hundred dollars on a fly reel.* You can acquire perfectly good rods and reels that will handle anything from big sharks and Tarpon to Bluegills for that or less. The reasons for purchasing anything more expensive become entirely aesthetic. The looks, the feel, the prestige – these types of factors are valid motivators for purchasing more expensive tackle. They have nothing to do with how it works. Look at it like this: a forty dollar Timex will keep excellent time and may last a lifetime, and so will a ten thousand dollar Rolex. The Rolex is a piece of jewelry. The Timex is a tool. I won't tell anyone they shouldn't pay ten grand for a Rolex, but I'll laugh at anyone who suggests it will keep better time than a forty dollar Timex. The simple fact is that you can buy fly rods and reels that will be more than up to the challenge of catching trophy bass for many years for much less than I mentioned above. Realistically, that bottom dollar number is probably around two hundred dollars for a quality rod, reliable reel, and top quality fly line – combined. You might be able to save money buying used tackle.

## Fly Rods for Bass Fishing

Once again, the framework of our discussion about fly rods will be predicated upon what works best for catching Largemouth Bass over four pounds, Hybrid and Striped Bass over seven pounds, and White Bass over three pounds in East Texas fisheries. Certainly, there are places in the country where Striped Bass grow to four times the size of their land-locked Texas cousins, but we're not concerned with them. Essentially, we are basing our discussion on two hypothetical fish: the ten pound Largemouth, Striper, or Hybrid, and the three pound White Bass. This requires a minimum of two different fly rods.

I'm also not going to tell you which rod action is best for you. So I won't be picking your brand or model for you. You should select a rod action that best suits your casting style and the type of fishing you are doing. People who argue about whether you need a fast action graphite rod or a much slower fiberglass or bamboo rod based on how the rod will perform when setting hooks or playing fish have such a limited knowledge of fly-fishing that they really shouldn't be giving advice...or they're trying to sell you something. The only exceptions are when targeting very soft-mouthed fish like Crappie and Trout when using very fine tippets and tiny flies, and when switching from a floating to a sinking line. In delicate presentation trout fishing, it actually will keep you from breaking off some fish if you use a more flexible rod. The rod will instantly absorb the shock of a surging or shaking fish, preventing some thrown flies, bent hooks, and broken tippets. Otherwise, it's all the same. As for sinking lines, a good rod needs to have a little more backbone and should not have a dramatically softer tip. A soft tip or slow action fly rod will slow your response time and reduce your lifting power with deeply submerged flies, leaders, and lines. A rod that is too flexible will force you to exert more energy to get the heavier line out of the water and into the air.  But you don't want a rod that is so stiff that you cannot feel what's happening, either.  A lot of modern fast action rods have a tip flex taper, meaning the tip section is very flexible while three quarters of the rod is very stiff.  This makes effectively fishing sinking lines more difficult due to the tip flexing every time the rod is the least bit out of alignment with the line, which eliminates your ability to feel a fish pick up your fly – especially if the fish is coming toward you when it takes.

When fishing sinking lines, you want to keep the rod as parallel to the fly line as possible by pointing the rod to the place where the fly is located.  This often means that your tip will be underwater.  Getting the rod out of alignment to the fly line will result in rod load every time you strip in some line.  Your nervous system is only capable of processing one sensation at a time.  This is the entire basis of a whole range of pain management therapies.  A TENS unit is a modern pain management device that relieves pain because the electrical impulses send a tingling sensation through your skin to your brain via nerves. Left on for a period of time, the brain begins to ignore the pain and focus on the tingling. For quite some time after the stimulation is removed, the brain will still not feel pain. It will "remember" the tingling. In the same way, your rod hand will send signals to your brain about the rod twitching when you strip line. If a fish strikes while the rod tip is loading or unloading, you'll never feel it. And since you spend so much time repeating the stripping motion and feeling the recurring "bounce" in the rod tip, you are conditioning your nervous system to ignore other sensations. I can't stress how important this concept is to effectively fishing sub-surface flies; and the deeper you are fishing the more important this becomes. A somewhat stiffer fly rod with a fairly stiff tip will give you a broader window of deflection from the perfectly parallel alignment before this tip bouncing phenomenon begins to happen. It will also help you apply more pressure to deeper fish, wearing them down and bringing them shallow in less time.

But don't think that means "the stiffer the better!" You're going to have to find a happy medium that works best for you. My main point here is to keep the rod pointed straight at the fly. The second point is that a tip flex rod will create problems in this regard. Good rods for sinking line applications will still have a smooth progressive taper, but will be stiffer than the rod you may prefer for fishing on or near the surface.

I've heard people say they want a stiff rod for "pulling bass out of the weeds" and such more often than I care to remember. *No fly rod is made for man-handling trophy-size fish.* Fly rods are made for casting essentially weightless flies. For this reason, they are more akin to a buggy whip than they are to a lever. *Any difference in rod stiffness that would enable a fly angler to muscle a big bass out of thick cover would make the rod nearly impossible to cast.* So dispel yourself of this myth right now. If you cast a slow action bamboo rod further and more accurately with less fatigue than you do a fast action graphite rod, then...by all means...use it! The accuracy of your cast and the raw number of casts you make will have far more to do with what you catch than any minor difference in what is currently referred to a "lifting power" or "fish-fighting power" in marketing literature. Furthermore, anyone who is using a fly rod to set the hook on big bass is a fool. You need to set the hook with a strip-set, rod pointed straight at the fly. So that negates the notion that a stiffer rod makes for a quicker and more powerful hook set. No it doesn't. No rod-based method of setting the hook compares to a strip-set in either speed or power. *When setting the hook on trophy bass, the rod is irrelevant.* We'll talk more about hook-setting and playing fish in a later chapter.

## The Ten Pound Bass Rod

Largemouth, Stripers, and Hybrid Bass are all trophies at ten pounds, or somewhere between twenty-five and twenty-eight inches in length. One rod can do the job on all three species in East Texas. Furthermore, this rod will also serve well for sight-fishing to Redfish on the Texas Coast. Ideal length will range from eight to nine feet. I don't think it matters which. That's a matter of personal preference based on your own casting style and fishing conditions. I've fished rods of various lengths between the two with great effectiveness, and I don't think there's much difference in the way an eight or nine foot rod performs on the water. I know some anglers believe that the extra foot of rod makes a big difference in whether or not their back cast hits the water, but I disagree. If you're hitting the water with an eight foot fly rod, you'll hit it almost as often with a nine foot fly rod. That's a flaw in the casting stroke. It's not the rod's fault. Eight foot rods seem to be long enough to mend line and all the other silly things we do with our fly rods where length matters, but the nine foot might be just a touch better. On the other hand, the eight foot rod will store and transport in a bit tighter spaces. I think the differences are too small to bother worrying about. My current bass rods are nine feet long eight weight St. Croix Legend Elites.

The line weight recommendation of the rod should be somewhere between a seven and a nine weight. I personally prefer eight weights for almost all trophy bass fishing. The line weight range is really a matter of the size of flies you're going to be casting and retrieving with the rod. It has very little to do with anything else. If I do find myself fishing deep with sinking lines and weighted flies (especially in current), I may grab my ten weight. But that's very, very unusual. Personally, I cast a lot of flies for trophy bass that are too heavy for a seven weight to control comfortably. Add a sinking line, and the seven weight is a bit light, making the amount of effort I must add to the equation skyrocket. This wears me out faster than had I fished with the eight weight to begin with. But there are some situations in which a seven weight would be ideal. All in all, I find that at least eighty percent of my trophy bass fishing is well-suited to an eight weight. And it is also my rod weight preference for Redfish on the coast. So that works out nicely.

I have fished these size rods in bamboo, fiberglass, and carbon fiber. I have found them all to work fine, but I want one with a progressive taper that flexes into the butt section of the rod with a medium-fast action. That matches up well to my casting stroke. I want a rod that has some tip sensitivity so that I can feel what's going on in the water. But I don't like stiff rods with floppy tips, and there are a lot of those on the market today. Essentially, you need an eight weight rod that you can cast accurately to about seventy feet all day long without wearing yourself out. That'll provide you with enough of a rod shopping challenge.

In recent years, a couple of brands have begun to market rods that are supposedly ideally suited to fly-fishing for Muskie, Pike, and trophy Bass. The rods are usually just under eight feet long, because of the tournament bass fishing rules of several sanctioning bodies that limit rod length to under eight feet. There is no other reason for making a seven foot eleven inch fly rod. They advertise the "lifting power" of these rods to "pull big fish out of cover" and tout their superior ability to "cast big, wind-resistant flies." I've cast several of these rods, and they've all been horrible. They're so stiff that they don't cast well, and certainly not at any distance or for roll casts. Distance casting of heavy and wind-resistant flies requires a *smooth* transfer of power from the rod to the line. These rods are anything but smooth. Furthermore, they're all tip heavy. That makes them a real chore to cast and fish. They're not well balanced at all, and that adds to swing weight; the leading cause of fatigue. The proper arrangement of the tools in fly casting is from heavier and thicker to lighter and thinner – from the caster to the fly. A rod that is tip heavy interferes with the smooth transfer of energy, creating inefficiency. Frankly, the reason the tips on these rods are so heavy is because the rods are so short and stiff that a normal tip would break off of them under normal fishing use. Finally, these rods are touted as being "perfect" for bass fishing because bass fishing...supposedly...consists of making a bunch of short, accurate casts with bulky flies. Well, I beg to differ! My average cast when hunting trophy bass is by no means "short." I typically cast at least sixty feet away from my location, and quite frequently make seventy foot casts. If a big Largemouth Bass knows you're there, he will *not* eat! If you believe that a thirty foot cast is all you need to catch lunker Largemouth consistently, good luck! You better be fishing in the dark. I've watched big bass sit and stare at my fly for as much as two minutes before inhaling it. And I've spent as much as an hour and a half trying to entice a big Largemouth to strike to no avail when I knew he could see me. The entire sales pitch for these so-called "bass fly rods" makes no sense to me. And I caught my first trophy Largemouth when I was barely a teenager – some three decades ago – on a borrowed bamboo fly rod sitting in an old wooden row boat about fifty feet from the bank with an old man who had been doing it all of his life. That was on Lake Holbrook in 1980, one of those smaller East Texas lakes I told you about earlier.

## *The White Bass Rod*

Your White Bass rod is going to be much lighter, but in the same length range. A five or six weight fly rod will be perfect for your White Bass fishing. You could probably get by with some four weights. Mine is a nine foot five weight medium action rod, the St. Croix Avid, but I used to catch a lot of White Bass on a fast action six weight when I fished for them in streams with more current.

The most effective flies for White Bass are light to medium weighted buck tail and marabou streamer flies like the Clouser Deep Minnow. These flies are light enough for a five or six weight fly rod, even when paired with a sink tip or sinking fly line. They're roughly the same size as a Crappie jig and work on the same principle, but are considerably lighter. We'll talk more about this later, but some mention needed to be made now to explain the type of rod that works best for catching big White Bass.

A trophy size White Bass will put up a fight on a much heavier rod, particularly in a stream with current. So you're in for some sporty fights on a five weight rod when you get in to the three pound Whites. Once again, the goal is to stay connected to the fish and keep moderate pressure on them at all times. They will wear themselves out. Since we don't often catch them in standing cover or around structures, you'll find that just keeping the rod bent long enough is all that it takes. So your trusty trout rod may work fine to fill this spot in your arsenal.

## *The Ten Pound Bass Reel*

A lot of today's younger or less experienced fly-fishermen will tell you that you need a reel with a powerful, smooth drag for trophy bass fishing. That's not really true. It certainly won't hurt to have a saltwater grade reel on that eight weight fly rod, but it isn't necessary for Largemouth Bass. Now, for Stripers and Hybrid Bass, it is more likely to come in handy. Here's why...

Lefty Kreh, has often said, "Any fish worthy of the drag on a fly reel will get there all by himself." What Lefty means is that anglers should play fish by hand if possible, and if the fish needs to be played on the reel it will force that situation upon you. You don't need to worry about it. And you certainly don't intentionally reel up the slack line below your last stripping guide while you have a fish on the hook. I've seen far more fish come unbuttoned while anglers tried to "put them on the reel" than I have ever seen landed that way. *Don't do it!* A fish against which you need the advantages of a quality drag will take all of your slack line in spite of your best efforts to keep him from it. And in my three decades of fly-fishing, I've had only about five freshwater fish ever do that to me. For the most part, when fishing freshwater, the reel is primarily a place to store unused fly line and backing. So how much do you want to pay for a big game quality drag? It's up to you. And if you plan to use this same rod and reel in saltwater, I'd highly advise you step up and get a good reel. Good saltwater reels start at two hundred dollars and go up to over a thousand. There are plenty of great ones for under five hundred dollars. Frankly, for an eight weight rod, there is no reason to spend more than four hundred bucks.

If you do step up to a big game grade fly reel, be sure to get one with a sealed, zero-maintenance drag. These are far superior to the old-fashioned open drags with cork, felt, and carbon pads that need constant and meticulous cleaning and oiling. Furthermore, take a good hard look at some of the newer "max arbor" designs. These reels stay cooler during high-speed operation (a long, blistering run from a worthy predator fish), pick up more line per turn of the handle, and in some cases weigh no more than a standard sized arbor design. They also don't kink fly lines stored on the reel for months or years on end. Because I use my eight weight rods for both fresh and saltwater fly-fishing, I do use high quality, max arbor, sealed drag fly reels milled from aircraft grade aluminum bar stock. They cost about three hundred fifty dollars each. I have two of them, with an extra spool for sinking lines for each rod. The only caveat to this whole reel discussion is that some of the modern big game style reels will not fit well (or at all) on old-fashioned reel seats that are often found on bamboo and vintage glass fly rods. When using vintage rods, you are usually well served by matching them to vintage reels.

If you don't fish saltwater and are only targeting big bass in fresh water you can certainly get by with a much less expensive reel that balances your rod and will hold somewhere near a hundred yards of backing and a floating fly line of the right weight rating. Brand new, these reels are going to start at about sixty dollars and you should not pay more than a hundred and fifty for one unless you want something pretty. The brands and models are too numerous to mention, but I've found reels from Okuma, Lamson, TFO, Echo, and several reels from Cabela's and L.L. Bean to be very reliable "economy class" freshwater reels.

## The White Bass Reel

For White Bass, you don't need to spend much on a fly reel at all. You can if you want to. But a fifty dollar fly reel on your five or six weight will do the job just fine. One of my personal favorites in the low-end-consumer reel category for light and mid-weight fly tackle is the Okuma Cascade. This is a reel that is manufactured from high-tech composite materials instead of metal. It has stainless steel internal gears with a low-maintenance nylon drag system of a center pin disc design. The reels are light enough to balance most fly rods, incredibly rugged and reliable, and ugly as sin. They are large arbor designs. They cost about twenty five to forty dollars. So you can buy a bunch of spare spools for different types of fly lines and still not spend a hundred dollars on a reel. Spare spools are important for bass fishing of all types, because you will want both floating and sinking fly lines for fishing different depths and presentations. I own some five weight fly reels that cost about three hundred dollars, but I'm just as comfortable fishing with these thirty dollar reels. In fact, I have a four weight St.

Croix Avid loaded with an Okuma Cascade in my trailer right now that I use for bream and trout fishing. Remember: the reel is mostly just a place to store unused line.

## *The Straight Line on Fly Lines*

There is a lot of confusion out there regarding fly lines. I'm not going to explain it all to you here, but I will tell you what you need to know about fly lines for bass fishing. As I said before, you're going to need a floating line and a sinking line – at the bare minimum. This means you will need two spools for your reel, or two rod and reel combos. Ideally, having a rod and reel rigged with a floating line and another rigged with a sinking line in the boat with you at the same time is the best solution. Sometimes, I choose to save space in the boat by carrying a spare spool with a sinking line on it instead of two complete rod and reel outfits. Sometimes, I'm carrying a rod and reel for bream fishing and a rod and reel for bass fishing. In that case, I carry a spare spool for the heavier rod and one for the lighter rod. I may rig up initially with either the floating or sinking lines.

Either way, the other line is on a spare spool in the boat if not rigged up on separate rods. If I have enough space in the boat, I'll rig four rods when fishing East Texas lakes: an eight weight with a floating line, an eight weight with a sinking line, a four weight with a floating line, and a five weight with a sinking line. The first two are for Largemouth, Stripers, and Hybrids. The four weight with a floating line is for Sunfish in shallow water along the banks. The five weight with a sinking line is for White Bass, bream in deeper water at certain times of the year, and for Channel Catfish. On rare occasions, I'll put a ten weight in the boat with a fast sinking line instead of the lighter rods. That's mostly for fishing very deep water (more than fifteen feet) for Largemouth and Hybrid Bass. Every now and then, I'll catch a Catfish or a Drum on that rig while bouncing flies slowly along the bottom.

Floating lines are common and relatively self-explanatory. But I want to mention a few of the finer points. First, there are a few good fly line companies out there that all make top quality fly lines. They each make lines that hit a range of price points from about twenty dollars to about a hundred dollars. In fly lines, you usually do get what you pay for. But a twenty five dollar fly line from a quality manufacturer will work just fine. Their one hundred dollar fly line will usually do the same job better. Rio, Scientific Anglers, Airflo, and Royal Wulff all have an excellent array of top quality fly lines. My personal favorites are Royal Wulff and Airflo lines, but I'd be content with high quality lines from any of these companies. I avoid store brand fly lines like the plague. I try not to buy lines from anyone who doesn't actually make fly lines. I've fished with and cast some good ones, but it's impossible to know what to expect. I've also run across some really crappy ones. But I've actually been fishing with a number of guys who were using OEM fly lines (lines made by one company to be branded for another company) who have had them disintegrate – coating ripping off, core breaking, welded loops breaking, etc. – on the water shortly after purchasing them. Inevitably, these lines were purchased for a few dollars less than a name brand fly line within the past couple of months. The poor guy may have saved ten dollars at the time of purchase, but now he's done fishing for the day and is still going to end up buying a better quality line. In reality he's out the thirty or forty dollars he spent on that crappy fly line and didn't save a dime. I own some name brand lines that are twenty years old. If you take care of a good fly line, it should last for many years.

For your floating lines, I recommend a high-end line from any of those manufacturers marketed as a "bass taper." But let me explain what a "bass taper" actually is. This is a minor modification to the standard weight forward or triangle taper fresh water fly line. The head of a weight forward fly line consists of a heavy end with both front and rear tapers and a short tip. These front and rear tapers can be of varying lengths for different applications. Each change causes the line to turn over a bit differently. In the case of a bass taper, the front taper and tip are cut back to the minimum length necessary, allowing the line to easily turn over much heavier and bulkier flies. Some manufacturers also over-weight the head of a bass taper line by a half or nearly full line weight. So an eight weight bass taper is likely to be an eight-and-a-half weight forward fly line with a very short front taper. The back taper may also have been shortened somewhat, but not nearly as dramatically as the front taper. Shortening the back taper can allow some weight forward fly lines to load the rod more efficiently with less line beyond the rod tip. This is useful for making quick re-casts after the pick-up, in particular reducing the number of false casts required to load the rod. In bass fishing, we're often blind casting and fan casting to cover an area or fish around a specific object. We make at least three times more casts than the sight-fisherman, who is casting to a fish he can see. Fewer false casts and less line in the air improves your endurance (in terms of hours of activity). This can make a big difference! The shorter total head length also allows you to retrieve more line before picking it up off the water, thereby keeping your fly in the water longer. I don't actually find this all that useful most of the time. I'll tell you why in a later chapter.

A line doesn't necessarily have to be marketed as a "bass taper" for it to actually be a weight forward floating line with a short front taper. But most manufacturers explain the head configurations of their fly lines in great detail in their marketing literature. For your information, the lines marketed as "Redfish" lines are generally the same head configuration as a bass taper, but the coating on the fly line is of the tropical saltwater variety. An integrated shooting head fly line is similar to a "bass taper," but even more severe in terms of the reduced rear taper and over-weight head. They generally have extremely short front tapers. The integrated shooting head is designed to virtually eliminate the need for false casting while making long fly casts. They can be useful in bass fishing in certain conditions. For example, I like using them when fishing from the shore. I will also use them if I know I'm going to be tangling with some stiff wind and need to make long casts. The integrated shooting head, like its cousin the traditional shooting head, requires a well-timed double haul to be really effective.

Keep that in mind if you aren't comfortable with your double haul technique.

The tropical saltwater coating on a fly line makes it stiffer than its freshwater counterparts. But no harm comes from using a saltwater fly line in fresh water. There are a few fly lines made for cold saltwater, which means saltwater with temperatures below seventy degrees. These are made primarily for Striped Bass fishing on the East Coast of the USA, but they can come in handy in other situations as well. A standard fly line will "wilt" in sub-tropical heat, making it sticky to the touch (hard to retrieve) and too limp to carry heavy flies in the air. A cold water fly line will wilt in water over seventy degrees. A tropical fly line will not wilt in the extremely hot marine environments of the tropics and sub-tropics, but it will usually kink up like a Slinky in water less than seventy degrees. *In the dog days of Summer on big East Texas lakes, I often switch to my tropical saltwater fly lines when fishing for bass.* The ambient temperatures on the deck of a boat and in the water are pretty similar whether I'm in the Florida Keys or on Lake Fork in July and August. In fact, it's actually about twenty degrees cooler in Key West! At a time like this, you want a fly line designed for sight-fishing to Redfish in tropical waters.

That's enough about floating lines. The really complicated stuff is sinking lines! Don't despair. I'll try and simplify this down to two choices and why I recommend one over the other.

There are basically two types of sub-surface fly lines: the sink tip fly line and the full sinking fly line. You need to understand that "full sinking" is not synonymous with "fast sinking." This is critical. A full sinking fly line is made in a way that allows the entire fly line to sink. A sink-tip fly line is a floating fly line with a weighted head that sinks. Generally speaking, this is the first twenty to thirty feet of fly line. The remainder floats on the surface. Full sinking fly lines come in a variety of sink rates; the speed at which a fly line sinks. They range from *Intermediate* (a very slow sink rate) to *Express* (almost a foot per second). Intermediate full sinking fly lines will sink at a rate of one half to one inch per second without a fly attached. Now, the same is true for sink tip fly lines. They have a range of sink rates from barely at all to pretty darned quick. Here's the problem:

Any fly below the surface that is ultimately connected to your rod tip via a piece of floating fly line will rise in the water column immediately when tension is applied to the line. If this tension is added by current, wind, rod tip motion, or retrieving of the fly line, the result is the same. The fly rises in the water column. In moving water, this fact of physics can be mitigated by mending the line upstream to reduce current tension, or accelerated with a downstream mend that increases current tension on the floating portion of the line. Sink tip fly lines can be useful for achieving specific presentations in moving water. *In my opinion, sink tip lines are counter-productive for fishing below the surface in still water in all situations relevant to trophy bass fishing.*

If I'm fishing below the surface, I want the fly to stay pretty close to the same depth I allow it to sink to until I'm ready to pick it up and cast again. You can only achieve this with a full sinking line. If you are fishing deep, you are doing so because that is where the fish are feeding. It may be four feet or ten feet. Either way, keeping the fly at four or ten feet longer is to your advantage. A sink tip may allow the fly to sink to four feet (and not much more), but as soon as you retrieve any line it begins to rise toward the surface. It will actually come up faster than it comes in. This isn't good. You want the fly to swim at that same depth throughout the target area. To do this, *you need a full sinking fly line*. Only if you actually want the fly to dart up toward the surface and then sink back down as you pause would you want to consider using a sink tip fly line. Now, this can be a very seductive presentation in certain circumstances. It works very well on White Bass using Clouser Deep Minnows. But here's the rub: you can do it with a heavy Clouser Minnow and floating line with a long leader. You don't need a sink tip fly line. I almost never fish for White Bass with anything other than a floating line. Notice I said "almost?" I'll explain that in a later chapter. *For now, what you need to understand is that a full sinking line is superior for bass fishing versus a sink tip fly line.* Many people of modest casting skill would much rather fish with a sink tip because they're easier to pick up. But that doesn't mean it's a more effective way to fool big bass into biting. Picking up a deep or heavy fly on a full sinking line is a two-step process. You execute a roll cast to bring the fly up near the surface, then pick it up with a back cast immediately. Most people don't know that, or they are simply too lazy to prefer a solid presentation over ease of casting. Trust me, they're missing a whole lot of quality fish by making that choice; particularly in the hottest and coldest times of the year.

How fast should your sinking line sink? That depends entirely on how deep you want to fish. The less time you spend counting a fly down to a specific depth, the more time you spend presenting the fly to fish at the right depth. I prefer not to over-weight my flies to make them sink faster. It's better to use a faster sinking line. But know this: in a pinch, you can put a heavier fly on a slower sinking line and it will sink much faster. In fact, I can put a really heavily weighted fly on an Intermediate sinking line and it will sink almost as fast as a fast sinking line. For this reason, the Intermediate sink rate is the most versatile. If you're only going to carry one with you, that's the one to go with. Ideally, I like to carry rigged rods and reels with a floating line, intermediate sinking line, and fast or express sinking line when I think I may need to search the entire water column between the surface and twenty feet deep. When I do this, I carry a pair of eight weights with the floating and intermediate lines along with a ten weight with the fast sinking (or Express) line. If I'm going to fish that deep, I'm going big or going home!

## Speaking of Leaders

One last note on the topic of sinking lines for bass fishing: shorten your leader down to no more than five feet. Three feet will usually suffice on a sinking line. Sometimes, you may want four. If I put five feet of leader on there, it's because I expect to lose some flies. But the longer your leader is, the less control you have over fly depth and the more difficult setting the hook becomes. Bass are not line shy. A few feet is sufficient at depths where light is becoming heavily refracted.

With a floating line, your ideal leader length is determined by an equation that includes the following variables: Light, Turbidity, Vegetation, and Wind. Keep the following ideas in mind:

- The brighter the sunlight, the lighter and longer your leader should be.
- The clearer the water is, the lighter and longer your leader should be.
- The thicker the vegetation is that you're fishing in, the shorter and heavier your leader should be.
- The windier it is, the shorter and heavier your leader should be.

Then add this footnote: Fishing in thick vegetation, use a smooth tapered leader with as few knots as possible. I carry a bunch of eight foot tapered Big Game leaders that terminate in twenty pound test for fishing to Largemouth Bass and Redfish in thick vegetation. I will remove a perfectly good leader with a tippet tied onto it and put on a brand new smooth one when I head into the thick stuff. Grasses, Lily Pads, and most other emergent vegetation will hang on those knots between leader and tippet. This *will* cost you big fish in the grass and pads! A knot at the fly and a knot at the fly line to leader connection are already two knots more than ideal. *Don't make it worse.* This is one of those fine points that is often the difference between a landed ten pound bass and "the one that got away!"

For floating lines, my standard bass fishing leader is seven or eight feet long. This is plenty for clear water. My leaders in clear water terminate in twelve pound test. My leaders in murky water terminate in sixteen or twenty pound test. If I'm fishing in snag-prone areas from a boat, I go with no more than twelve pound test tippet. I want to be able to break it if I get

snagged deep below the surface. If you aren't a very

experienced fly-fisherman that might sound backwards. You

might think you'd want heavier leader that will withstand more

abrasion and more pounds of pressure if you're fighting big fish

in snag-filled waters (like submerged trees and stumps or a rip-

rap bank). If I'm fishing in shallow water around emergent

structure, that's true. But when I am concerned about getting

snagged on something substantial several feet below the

surface, I must be able to break the tippet by pulling on the fly

line with my hand from a boat. I cannot use a fly rod to exert

enough force. It just won't do it. That's a great way to break a

rod! I may not be able to free it with a boat paddle, etc. If I

cannot break the tippet by pulling on the fly line bare-handed,

then I am likely to be forced to cut my fly line. That will cost me

at least seventy dollars! I'll give up a few flies and a few good

fish now and then to keep from spending an extra seventy

bucks on a fairly regular basis. If the stakes were high enough in

some tournament or a personal bet, I guess I may reconsider

and go with the heavier tippet and leader.  But that's a bizarre hypothetical situation I never expect to confront.

Buy the very best tippet and leader material you can convince yourself that you can afford.  Make no mistake about it, there is a "clearly the best" when it comes to tippet and leaders for fly-fishing.  That's Seaguar Grand Max.  The only thing I don't use it for is a floating leader for fishing dry flies for trout and pan fish.  My second choice is Rio Fluoroflex.  I use Rio Powerflex for dry fly fishing, because Nylon floats better than fluorocarbon (and it's a lot cheaper).  Fluorocarbon has proven to me and nearly every angler I respect that it is so superior to nylon when fishing below the surface that it is worth paying two to three times as much for it.  I won't bother you with a lengthy explanation of why or how.  I'll just say emphatically: *if you want to catch trophy fish on a fly, you better have some top quality fluorocarbon tippet material!*

Many warm water fly-fishermen do not bother themselves with tapered leaders at all.  Instead, they fish with a straight piece of monofilament or fluorocarbon line tied between the fly and the fly line. This gets into that category of making things tougher (and cheaper) on yourself than actually improving your odds. Tapered leaders turn flies over better and more easily. It's that simple. You'll hear guys say, "Well, I just use a straight piece of twelve pound mono, and I've never had a problem." That may be entirely true. But I guarantee you that same guy could make the same casts with less effort if he used good tapered leaders. If he uses less effort, he could make more casts...and more accurate casts. And you already know what I think about the ratio between number of presentations to fish and fish caught. But if there was only one corner to be cut in pursuit of trophy bass, this might be it. Since leader lengths are fairly short, diameters are relatively big, flies are relatively bulky, and bass are not typically line shy, the difference between a tapered leader and a flat leader on the end of a bass tapered fly line is arguably not worth fussing about...until you find yourself in a situation where you need a long, light leader due to bright light and water clarity – and the fact that the bass are whacking Dragonflies on the surface.

## *The Weak Link*

If we have all the right gear, find the bass, go to them, and present them with an irresistible fly, the good news is they are very likely to take it. But all of that effort will come to naught if we hook big bass after big bass and cannot bring them to the boat. The whole point of catching trophy bass is to actually land them. Once you hook one, you've still got a lot of variables in the equation that will factor heavily into whether or not you actually land one. At this point, one of the weakest links in the chain between you and that trophy fish is the knot you've tied. We're talking about the line to leader knot, any leader to tippet knots, and the tippet to fly knot. The fewer knots there are between you and that fish, the better your odds. At the minimum, you're going to have a line to leader knot and a leader to fly knot. To improve your chances of successfully landing this big bass, you must tie high quality fishing knots. If you want some insurance, you can glue those knots with a special glue such as UV Knot Sense. Do not, under any circumstances, use any type of Super Glue! You can use a dab of some of the various light-cured resins in their flexible version, such as Tuffleye Flex. But many solvent-based glues will actually turn your fly line and leader material brittle. While the knot may not slip, it becomes easier to break. These light-cured flexible resins won't harm the fly line or leader. They won't make the knot brittle, but they'll lock it in place and prevent it from slipping. This will improve overall knot strength by reducing internal abrasion. But there is no such thing as a perfect knot. Perfect is a continuous piece of integrated material. Any time you form a joint, you create a weak spot.

There are entire books dedicated to arguments for and against every fishing knot ever invented. But there are some knots that have stood the tests of time with mariners, climbers, and fishermen alike. This list of proven knots is a bit shorter, especially once you eliminate all of the special purpose knots that are not appropriate for fishing. In fact, I only use four

fishing knots with any regularity at all. They are:

- Nail Knot – either a single or double version of this

  knot is sufficient for all but the most grueling of

  sport-fishing conditions like Marlin, Tuna, and

  Tarpon fishing. This knot is what I use to attach

  leaders to fly lines. Then I apply UV Knot Sense.

- Surgeon's Loop – either double or triple, I use this

  knot to connect leaders to tippet and to join two

  pieces of tippet. My rule of thumb is that I use a

  double Surgeon's Loop for line with a test strength

  of 10 lbs or greater, and I use a triple Surgeon's

  Loop for lines with a test strength of less than 10

  lbs. This is actually the most finicky of the knots I

  tie. You need to take great care to get these knots

  tied properly. If you do, they will rarely ever fail. It

  has almost as much strength as the lighter piece of

  line being joined.

- No-Slip Loop Knot – I tie most flies to the leader or tippet using this knot. It's a very strong, durable knot that allows the fly to dangle freely at the end. This allows the fly to have a more life-like action in the water. Virtually all of my bass flies are connected using this knot with only a few exceptions. If I am fishing in weed beds I do not use it, because the open loop ahead of the eye of the hook creates yet one more thing that a weed stem can cling to. I don't use it for bass poppers.

- Improved Clinch Knot – In the weeds, this is my knot for attaching a fly to the leader. It creates a smooth barrel at the top of the hook eye that doesn't snag easily, but it does stifle the motion (or action) of the fly a bit. I use this knot to attach dry flies and poppers. Dry fly fishing relies entirely upon a visual presentation, and this knot has a very slim profile. The action of poppers is actually improved by the added stiffness at the leader to fly connection.

If you master these four knots, you are as ready as you can be for catching trophy bass. If you tie them sloppily, no one can help you. You will lose more fish than you catch. That's a certainty.

You'll also hear anglers talk about how much money they save by "building their own" leaders. This means they take multiple pieces of leader material (or even plain old fishing line) and tie them together in decreasing diameters toward the fly end. They'll use a fairly heavy and stiff butt section that attaches to the fly line. Each piece thereafter must be lighter and shorter than the piece before it, or it will not turn over a fly efficiently. Any drastic change from heavy to light line will create a hinging effect as the leader turns over a fly. The forces of a fly cast can cause this joint to fail, snapping the fly off in mid-air. And no matter how you slice it, you've got more knots between you and the fish. *The fewer knots between you and the fish, the better your odds of landing him.* A good tapered bass leader will cost you two to four dollars. Bought in bulk, they can cost much less...and they'll store for years (especially fluorocarbon). So what's that hero shot with that trophy bass or your name in a record book worth to you? If it's not worth a couple of bucks, you'll probably never catch him.

In the next chapter, we'll talk about the tried and proven fly patterns that consistently produce trophy bass in East Texas. But I'm not going to try to create an exhaustive compendium of those that work. I'm going to give you a minimum combination that will cover every situation; the flies I consider the best of the bunch.

# *Chapter Five*

There are plenty of great books and articles written by far greater anglers than myself about what, when, and why bass eat what they do. The definitive book on the subject from the fly-fisherman's perspective is still Dave Whitlock's <u>L.L. Bean Fly Fishing for Bass Handbook</u>, first published by The Lyons Press in 2000. I've been fortunate enough to spend quite a bit of time with him and his wonderful wife, Emily. I've learned a lot from him, and Emily gave my wife her first casting lesson. But I grew up in the footprint of another master of Largemouth Bass fisheries management, Bob Lusk. You can't grow up with a fishing pole in your hand in East Texas without at least unwittingly reaping the benefits of Bob Lusk's genius. The man is a Texas A&M educated fisheries biologist who has spent his life studying Largemouth Bass, their habitats, their eating habits, and their breeding behavior and then teaching others to maximize the genetics and environmental factors most favorable to growing huge bass like no one else. The success of both his consultancy firm and his publication, *Pond Boss* magazine, are testaments to his expertise and to his ability to communicate that knowledge to laymen. *Pond Boss* magazine is the leading authoritative literary source for private fisheries management in the USA. Bob's focus isn't on *catching* huge bass. His focus is on *growing them* in their natural habitat.

> *Largemouth bass can eat another bass 50 percent of their body length. Imagine a 20-inch bass eating another 10-inches long. Those feeding habits develop at an early age. When stocking fingerlings in the spring, we've seen a three-inch bass with a slightly smaller cousin in his mouth. There's no way to consume it, but the attempt demonstrates a bass' ferocious predator instincts. Bass prefer big meals, not chasing small baitfish and wasting energy that could be converted to growth.* (Bob Lusk, *Bass Prefer Big Meals*; Did You Know? Bob Lusk Outdoors, July 31, 2011.)

This is the main reason why I fish for lunker bass with *huge* flies. Big bass become extremely efficient and aggressive predators by the time they're a foot long. By the time they become two feet long (a true trophy size bass), they've had years to refine their survival craft. They don't waste effort. They are masters of their own domains. They've figured out what works and what doesn't. They may not become highly selective about what they eat, but they get very selective about feeding mainly on large, protein-dense victims. They will mostly eat crayfish, shad, shiners, other sunfish, salamanders, and smaller bass. When you catch them feeding in shallow water, they will also eat small rodents and birds, water snakes, and frogs. But you are very unlikely to find big bass feeding shallow in clear water on a bright, sunny day. If the sky is clear in the summer-time, you're only going to find big bass feeding on or near the surface right at sunrise and in the deep shadows of late afternoon and evening.

The bass sees very similarly to how humans see, except that they view the world through a yellow filter. So try this experiment. Put on a pair of amber lens shooting glasses. That's how a bass sees the world around him. Go underwater and open your eyes. Now you're seeing what bass see. You'll notice that blues and violets are less intense, but greens are highlighted. Contrast between light and shadow are enhanced. Motion is easier to detect because of this intensification of contrast. Depth perception is improved when viewing the world around you through amber lenses. Light refracted or reflected through the water is also amplified. These things are going to play a key role in how we design or select our bass flies.

Size and visible cues aren't the only things we need to consider. We also have to pay close attention to the pressure changes caused by water displacement and sound waves, because the bass relies heavily upon its ability to sense even minute changes in pressure, vibration, and sound; both for foraging and for security. We want to choose flies that are the right size to ring Mr. Bass's dinner bell, and that displace enough water to make it easier for him to find them, that provide enough visual contrast for him to pick them out in his low-light world, and that give the right cadence and frequency of vibrations to suggest that this might be an easy meal.

The second reason I fish big flies when hunting for big bass is that I want to eliminate the by-catch of smaller fish. I want to attract the biggest bass in the pond, and scare off everything else. This is probably the most controversial thing I'm sharing with you in this book. I know I'm fishing a big enough fly when I see the tiny post-spawn fry jumping out of the water skittering away quickly to safety when I move the fly through the water. If Bluegill are hitting your fly, it isn't big enough. If bass under twelve inches are hitting your fly, it probably isn't big enough to motivate that ten pounder to strike. If you want to catch a twenty-five inch bass, you shouldn't be presenting a fly that a twelve inch bass will take. A twenty-five inch bass will eat a twelve inch bass if he's hungry, but a fifteen inch bass can't. So he won't try. Big bass eat medium-sized Bluegills (up to about ten inches long). Honestly, we simply can't cast flies that big. But we can cast flies that imitate six inch bait fish, frogs, and mice. So that's what we're going to do.

The smallest fly I will cast when I'm fishing for big bass is over four inches long. The largest I will fish with a seven or eight weight rod is about seven inches long and quite slender – usually an imitation of a water snake or salamander. With ten weight tackle, I can cast imitations of bait fish up to eight inches long. We're talking about flies tied on hooks that are from size two to size 3/0. I've often marveled at the fact that my flies for Largemouth Bass are almost as big as my box of Tarpon flies. The largest Largemouth Bass anyone has ever caught weighed a couple dozen pounds, but a good Tarpon weighs between one hundred and two hundred pounds. Yet, these fish prefer about the same size meals. With that said, I want the vast majority of my flies to be big enough to get Mr. Lunker's attention, but not so big that they're difficult to cast. Ninety percent of my bass flies are between four and six inches long so that I can cast them efficiently with an eight weight fly rod.

I'm going to be fishing my bass flies in thick cover, around, and in structure. So I make them as durable as humanly possible. Bass flies use a lot of expensive materials and large hooks. I want them to last for many fishing trips. Choosing patterns that can be made snag-resistant or weedless is a very good idea. I do not fish many patterns with a downward hook orientation unless they have a weed guard, because Largemouth Bass eat three fourths of their food near the bottom. This eliminates a lot of patterns from consideration for the vast majority of my bass fishing.

In short, you're going to want a selection of big bass flies that effectively imitates the most common foods of Largemouth Bass, including forage fish like shad and Bluegills, crayfish, frogs, lizards, and small water snakes. Then you might toss in a mouse. That will cover it and the flies will take up so much space that you will easily fill a big fly box with them. Each pattern should be tied in at least one natural, one dark, and one light color combination to account for different water turbidity and ambient light. And you will probably want to tie most of the sub-surface patterns in a light-weight and heavy version. For temperate bass, your fly selection will fixate exclusively on shad patterns. Since we'll fish these in open water instead of thick cover and heavy structure, the need to keep them snag-resistant or weedless is no big deal.

## *Largemouth Bass Flies*

Here is my list of "must have" flies for Largemouth Bass:

- Wool Head Muddler – I fish this fly in size 2 to size 1/0 when hunting for trophy bass. I carry them in a Bluegill color pattern consisting of olive over chartreuse wing with a red tail and olive wool head, a chartreuse and yellow version, and a black version. All of these get a double weed guard made of 12-16 lbs hard mono. I never add weight to this fly pattern, and it can be fished from near the

Wool Head Muddler Minnow in Yellow and Chartreuse

Wool Head Muddler in Bluegill Colors

surface to about six feet deep – or deeper on a fast sinking fly line. The fly imitates Bluegill, small bass, and big Fathead Minnows. The materials soak up water, making the fly sink better the longer you fish it. The marabou breathes when the fly is motionless, imitating the fine motion of gills and fins. When stripped, the marabou flattens out, but retains bulk. So the fly undulates with and without motion. The wool head displaces water when the fly is stripped, and sinks slowly when sitting still. This allows me to fish the fly very naturally – the way real forage fish move around in the water.

- Clouser Deep Minnow – I fish this fly for trophy bass in size 2 to size 2/0 and I carry them in green over white, chartreuse and white, black on black, black over chartreuse, and gray over white. For bass fishing, I tie all of them from natural bucktail and a bit of Crystal Flash. I tie them with both UV enhanced and regular flash, with the heaviest and

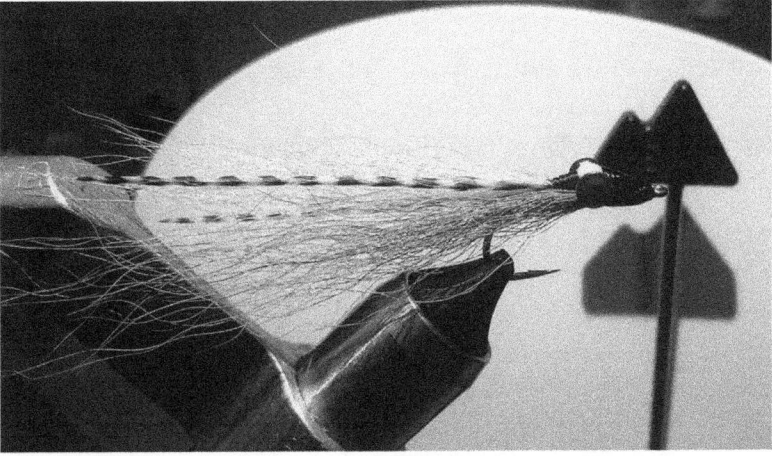

Clouser Deep Minnow variant in Gray over White

Another Clouser Deep Minnow variant

darkest ones getting UV flash. I do not like to over-weight these flies with excessively heavy dumb bell eyes. I prefer to use a moderate amount of weight and fish them with a sinking fly line when I need to go deep. This is a general rule of thumb I follow when fishing still water. If I'm fishing in significant current, then I use heavier eyes. The Clouser Deep Minnow imitates the profile of a bait fish and the jigging motion of wounded and disoriented forage fish. But it is a suggestive pattern, not a realistic one. When tied and fished properly, it is one of the most versatile and effective fly patterns in the history of fly-fishing for catching fish with a strong predatory instinct.

- Dahlberg's Diver – I tie them in various styles of tails including both feathers and rabbit strips. I mostly tie this fly for Largemouth Bass on a size 2 or size 1 hook so that I can fish them on my eight weight tackle. I tie a few big ones for the ten weight, but not many. I tie almost all of them in some combination of green, brown, yellow, and chartreuse. I add some orange to some of them for good measure. This fly also gets a double weed guard of mid-weight hard mono. I don't add flash or synthetic materials to these flies. They're all natural: deer hair, rabbit strips, feathers, and marabou. Sometimes, I add rubber legs. I really don't think it matters, except on the ones with tails built of feathers. I almost always tie in some rubber leg material to the tail on these to change the way the tail undulates in the water. Leave this fly sitting on the surface for up to a minute or more after casting it. Then twitch it once. Let it sit for another thirty seconds. Then twitch it three times. Let it sit still again for ten seconds. Then pick it up a re-cast it unless you see a bass moving toward it. This fly is a very life-like imitation of a frog when fished properly. Frogs don't swim on the surface. They

Dahlberg's Diver

swim just below the surface. On the surface, they sit still. Keep this in mind when fishing this fly, because the fly has a very froggy profile and moves just like one when fished well. Frogs don't usually swim very far without resting on the surface and they tend not to cover much distance between breaks. Most strikes from quality bass will come when the fly is resting on the surface.

- Deer Hair Popper – I tie them in frog green and yellow in sizes 2 to 1/0. I use a combination of rubber leg material and streamer feathers for the tail. They also get a double mono weed guard. I move them more than I do the diver fly above, but learn to make short, quick strips that don't move the fly more than a couple of inches at a time and still achieve the "pop" that they're named after.

- Cork Poppers – I tie these in sizes 1 and 1/0 with feather tails and a couple of rubber legs. I tie them in green and yellow, blue, and black. Again, these

Deer Hair Popper

Hard Body Popper

get weed guards like the rest. I really prefer deer hair poppers and divers most of the time, because I have found large bass in lakes and ponds very hard to fool into striking the hard body poppers. They're fine for smaller bass and on rivers. I keep these flies moving after the initial settling period following the cast. Let the rings die out. Pop once and pause. Let it sit for fifteen seconds. Then pop steadily until you're ready to cast again.

- Grinnel Flies – This is an old East Texas fly pattern that is relatively easy to tie and extremely effective when fished in and around weeds, particularly near the shore. It imitates small snakes and salamanders. It is the fly-fisherman's version of an un-weighted rubber worm or salamander rigged weedless. Natural deer hair and natural rabbit zonker strips with a mono weed guard tied on a size 4 or size 2 streamer hook. Trim the head slender

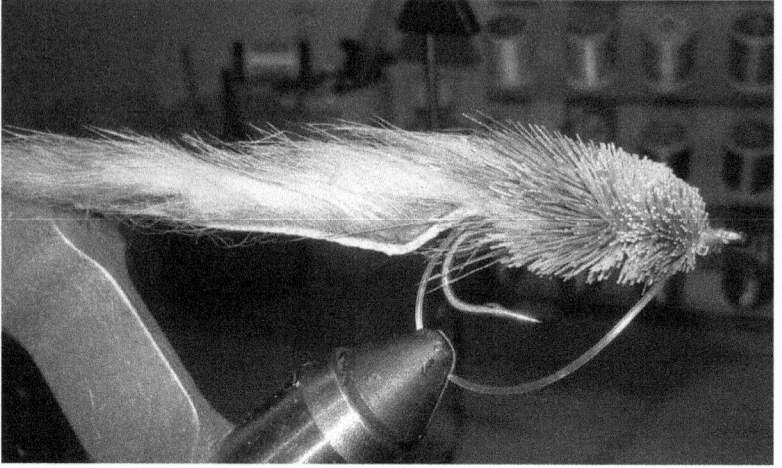

Grinnel Fly

(close to the hook shank).  Fished either floating or on an Intermediate sinking fly line, the big ole bass will whack the snot out of this fly during the Summer and Fall!  Fish it very slowly with long strips.  Try to make it look like a real water snake poking around.  Every now and then, make a short twitch with the fly resting on the surface.

- Wooly Buggers – We're talking BIG Wooly Buggers! Sizes 4 to 1, with and without bead heads or lead wire under-bodies for various weight and different presentations.  Imitates Hellgrammites, Hex Nymphs, salamanders, crayfish, and Catalpa Worms.  Yes, in East Texas, even large bass will eat Giant Hexagenia Nymphs in the rare places where this hatch occurs.  Look for muddy bottoms in shallow coves, sloughs, and ponds in about four feet of water.  Same goes for Catalpa Worms when they fall from the overhanging trees in Summer along shorelines.  I tie Bunny Buggers, Wooly Buggers with rubber legs, and Buggers with Estaz bodies and no hackle in a variety of configurations. The problem most fly anglers have with fishing Bugger style flies for Largemouth Bass is that they are way too small. Most folks fish them in size 6 to 10. That's fine for catching little bass and all the bream you can stand, but it won't get the time of day from a big ole Bucketmouth. Go big or go home! I tie them in color patterns ranging from black to rusty brown, and from olive to chartreuse; add legs and flash that compliment the base color. The chartreuse and yellow Bugger is tied with no weight, a short marabou tail make of black and chartreuse, and Cactus Chenille body in chartreuse. Then palmer an under-sized black feather over the body and counter-wrap with medium gauge wire. You can also use chartreuse Estaz and leave the feather off, but counter-wrap with medium black wire. The latter is my favorite. Be advised:

168

Assorted Buggers

Channel Catfish will also hit this fly when the worms are falling, sometimes executing violent surface takes. Nothing makes a more effective crayfish imitation than a rusty brown to sculpin olive Wooly Bugger with a bead head and two short rabbit strips splayed apart for a tail. You can tie this same pattern on a Gamakatsu SC15 using dumb bell eyes mounted further forward than on a Clouser Minnow to create a deadly and snag-resistant crayfish pattern that rides in the water with the hook point up. Bounce it along rocky ledges and around submerged stumps. There is no reason to get elaborate with crayfish patterns.

- Puglisi Minnows – This is the one pattern that I use for Largemouth Bass fishing that is a classic flat bait fish imitation with a downward oriented, exposed hook point. Why? Because this fly suspends excellently in the water column and provides an exceptionally convincing and sophisticated "life-like" look for bass in clear water. I can control the depth easily to keep it out of the grass on the bottom. I can cast it very precisely into holes no bigger than a trash can lid and fish it there for several seconds, or I can fish it over deeper beds – both bass and bream beds. I can fish this fly along the outside (deep) edge of weed beds. This fly enables the angler to fish a very delicate presentation with a fly that presents a big profile and stay in the strike zone for a very long time. I tie them to imitate Bluegills, shad, and Golden Shiners in sizes 4 – 3/0. For deeper water versions, I tie this fly using the "V" technique and glue-on eyes mounted right behind the hook eye and cemented with epoxy or Tuffleye. Rarely, I'll tie the largest ones with some lead wire wrapped around the hook shank for extra weight. Tied this way, the fly is bulkier, displacing more water when it is stripped, and the fly sinks quickly. It will also dart upward a

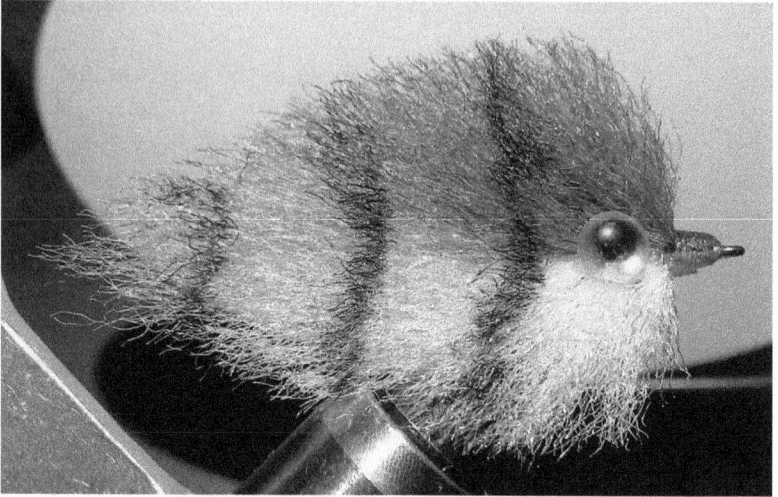

Puglisi Minnow in Bluegill colors

bit when stripped and then dip back down in the water column on the pause, imitating a forage fish that is either wounded or preoccupied with feeding on the edge of the grass. Bass are bullies, and they'll pick on both.

- Deer Hair Mouse – Tie them on a size 1 or size 2 hook so that the body of the mouse is 1 ½" to 2" long. The tail should be a shaved natural rabbit zonker strip. Natural deer belly hair makes a great mouse color fly made of real fur that will actually smell like a wet rat when you fish it. You can add chamois ears and black eyes if you feel the need, but the bass will never notice. Bass see them from underwater. Get the profile, tail, and whiskers right and you'll fool even the most wary bass that's hanging out near the bank at dusk or at night. I tie moose mane in for whiskers, and I tie them disproportionately long. Mice sometimes have amazingly long whiskers, and the extra life-like movement can't hurt.  Besides, they're going to get smashed and broken over time anyway.  The slower you fish a mouse fly, the more realistic it becomes.  Put a double weed guard on them and cast them up on the bank.  Then drag them into the water gently.

Deer Hair Mouse

## *Temperate Bass Flies*

This is pretty simple and two of the four patterns are listed above for Largemouth Bass. These are the only flies I use for Stripers, Hybrids, and White Bass:

- Clouser Deep Minnow – For Stripers and Hybrids, tie them in size 2 – 1/0 in gray over white, black over chartreuse, and olive over white with UV flash. For White Bass, tie them in size 4 in gray over white, black over chartreuse, and black over white with UV flash.

- Rabbit Strip Leech – Add some weight to get this pattern down, but don't over-do it. I tie them in white, black, and olive. For Stripers and Hybrids, tie them big. We're talking about size 2 – 3/0, with magnum zonker strips for the tail and no flash. For White Bass, tie them on a size 4 hook in white or gray. Use moderate weight and no flash. I have a slightly unusual way of tying these that gives them

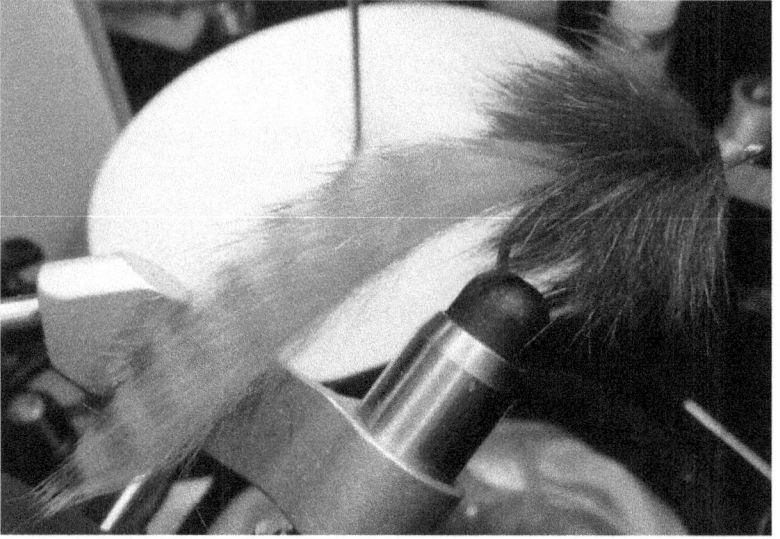

Bunny Leech

Right Rabbit

more of a bait fish profile. I call this fly the *Right Rabbit*. I tie them with a dark zonker and white or chartreuse cross-cut rabbit strip. I tie the zonker in for the tail using a mono loop to keep it from fouling and enough material to stretch all the way to the eye of the hook. Leaving that loose for a moment, I tie in the cross-cut rabbit strip and palmer it forward to behind the eye. Using wet fingers, I stroke all of the cross-cut strip fur downward toward the point of the hook. Then I pull the zonker forward over the hook shank and tie it in behind the eye. I build a thread head and apply a pair of stick-on eyes. Then I coat the head in Tuffleye or epoxy. It's very effective.

- Puglisi Minnows – Stripers and Hybrid Bass love big Puglisi Minnows fished on a sinking line almost as much as Tarpon do! I tie them in size 1 – 3/0, and about five to seven inches long. I tie them in black over chartreuse, purple over white, gray over white, and olive over white. UV enhanced material may give you an edge when fishing deep. For White Bass, tie them is size 4 and in gray over white and black over chartreuse to about three inches long. Temperate bass will hit them on the pause more often than not.

- Lefty's Deceiver – This is a feather and fur version of a flat bait fish minnow fly similar to the totally synthetic Puglisi Minnow. It will sink faster than a Puglisi Minnow, even when it is not weighted. I tie most of these with a bit of weight to them. This can include lead wire wraps, an epoxy thread head, or both. I use this fly most when fishing deeper than six feet, pairing it with a sinking fly line. I tie them from size 2 to size 3/0...from 3 to 7 inches long. You'll want a variety of Deceivers in white, chartreuse, purple, black, and green. I usually tie them in bi-color versions with a white belly and a colored wing, but I do tie some in solid chartreuse, purple, white, and black. The chartreuse version gets gold and chartreuse flash. The purple and black get gray or black olive UV flash. The white version gets silver and UV gray flash. I put high quality stick-on eyes on these and cover the head in Tuffleye or five minute epoxy. Nowadays, a lot of folks are into Deceivers tied with synthetic materials. You'll hear all kinds of claims about how they "move better in the water." Nothing...I repeat...*nothing* moves more naturally in the water than feathers, buck tail, and marabou! For a version that displaces a lot of water, tie some Fathead Deceivers. This is a Deceiver with a round, spun deer hair or wool head on the fly. Deer hair is more buoyant than wool. Wool soaks up water and gains a little weight. Both push water pretty darned well, and this fly...tied either way...will create quite a racket deep below the surface and present bass with a big bait fish profile and very life-like motion.

Lefty's Deceiver in Olive and White

- A white hard-bodied popper – size 2 to size 6. I fish this fly on a five or six foot long leader using a sink-tip or intermediate fly line. The sinking line will cause the floating popper to dive and re-surface when stripped. I fish with short strips and minimal pauses. They make a very seductive racket that convinces White Bass that a shad is dying on the surface. Strikes are usually pretty violent.

That's all you need. If you're presenting to active fish, they will eat one or more (sometimes any) of these. Choose your hooks wisely and keep them as sharp as humanly possible. I de-barb all of my hooks for several reasons. First, I don't want to get stuck by a barbed hook. Sooner or later, every fly-fishermen buries a fly in his own flesh. Second, studies have shown that barbless hooks penetrate significantly better than barbed hooks, requiring less pressure to set the hook. Third, it makes releasing landed fish much safer, easier, and quicker. That improves their survival rate. And all the worry of novices about barbless hooks falling out of a fish's mouth easier is pure hogwash if you keep a bend in the rod. So the benefits far outweigh any perceived negative.

## Bulletproofing Your Flies

I can't say enough about the increased satisfaction that comes from tying your own flies. It's not only the fact that you're catching fish on flies you tied yourself, although that makes a big difference to a lot of anglers. It's also about all of those stormy days that you can't go fishing. It's about having something to do in the evening after the kids go to bed to help you unwind – something that connects you to your fishing. It's about all of that down time at the office you can now spend tying up a couple of new bass flies. And it is about gaining a better understanding of the game, fine tuning your presentations to precisely the way you want them, and the ability to experiment with different patterns, colors, and weights of flies. All of this will make you a better angler.

If you tie your own flies, there are some things that I would advise you to do to make your flies infinitely more durable than the ones you buy at the fly shop or from the Internet. Several years ago, I got very serious about tying more durable flies – especially for bass fishing and saltwater fishing. The tips I'm giving you here are incorporated into every bass or saltwater fly that I tie. Some of these techniques go in to my trout flies, too. I've developed these habits through trial and error, systematic experimentation, and a lot of study. You can put a little bit more effort into your flies and have them last through dozens of fish and years of fishing, or you can ignore these tips in favor of cutting a few corners. It's entirely up to you. It doesn't matter to me. But I figured I'd share this information just in case someone else is as obsessed about keeping their fishing budget under control as I am. Here are the suggestions:

1. Don't be afraid of glue.

I put a slime of some sort of super glue on every single hook shank before I secure thread to it. I do not put glue on the portion of a hook shank that will be receiving spun deer hair or wool. Also be careful not to cover areas right below hair and feather wings that run parallel to the hook shank and are tied in at the head, as in a Clouser Deep Minnow. If I'm laying down a thread base, it gets a coat of penetrating Hard as Hull before I start the thread.

When I tie in tails and rubber legs, I reinforce them with a bit of penetrating Hard as Hull, Zap, or super glue. Hair wings are all secured with a dab of penetrating Hard as Hull at the tips before the thread wraps are applied. I brush the glue on the spot where the hair wing will be tied in. Then I add the clump of hair. Then I apply the thread wraps. If I'm doing a stacked hair wing (multiple colors or types of material in a single wing), then I apply the glue after applying each layer of thread wraps, too. Don't think this is somehow "unconventional" or "cheating," because I learned this from Bob Clouser and Dave Whitlock, two of the greatest fly tying experts and innovators of the past century.

When I finish a thread head on a fly, I apply penetrating Hard as Hull and let it dry. Then I go back over the thread head with High Set Head Cement, 5 minute epoxy, or Tuffleye. None...zero...of my flies ever come unwound. They usually rust or the hooks break before the materials and thread wear out.

When I tie in a weed guard, I glue under it and over the thread wraps that hold it to the hook shank. Then I glue the thread wraps at the hook eye. That's in addition to bending the weed guard tips back upon themselves and cinching them down with plenty of tight wraps of heavy duty tying thread.

When you're hitting trees, bushes, stumps, docks, concrete walls and walkways, and the occasional side of the boat with your flies, they need to be durable. Successfully catching a bunch of trophy bass will require a lot of very close casting to solid structure. The best casters in the world are going to hit stuff now and then. Big bass can be surprisingly hard on flies when you consider they don't have any dangerous teeth or crushers like many saltwater fish do. The inside of the mouth of a big, old Largemouth, Striper, or Hybrid Bass is full of plates of cartilage separated by flexible membranes. They can apply a surprising amount of pressure, as you'll soon discover if you ever let one close his mouth on your fingers. And their lips are covered with coarse grain that's just like sand paper. But more wear and tear will befall your flies from colliding with the thick cover and structure you find these fish in than anything the fish could do to it. Thoughtful use of good glue products and epoxy will pay for itself many times over in durability.

2. If I am tying in a material, I double it over the tie-in wrap. The only exception is really bulky stuff. When tying in a bulky material, I rely on the glue and quality thread wraps. But flash, many wing materials, virtually all roped materials (like chenille), and so forth all gets doubled over the initial thread wraps and then tied down. Most stuff gets glued, too.

3. Every time I change materials while tying a fly, I execute 2 half hitches to tie off the thread...and usually touch it with a bit of glue. Once again: my flies n-e-v-e-r come untied.

One reason for this is that I am a rotary fly tier. If you use the rotary feature of a vise to wrap materials the way it's intended to be used, you have to learn to half hitch off the stages of your flies as you tie them. Otherwise, they have a tendency to come undone on you at the most inopportune times. I can walk away from a half tied fly and come back days later to finish it without worrying about it coming unbuttoned while I'm away. But most importantly, if one portion of the fly fails, the rest of the fly is still intact. If I break the thread later in a pattern, I don't lose all of my work. I simply re-attach the thread and continue.

4. I use nothing but the highest quality materials I can find. I'd prefer to have less stuff of high quality than to have a bunch of stuff of suspect quality. I use nothing but Gamakatsu hooks and Danville thread. I use Tuffleye for about 90% of all epoxy applications. I spend a small fortune on high grade feathers, buck tail, and deer hair.

5. I counter-wrap most hackle feathers with wire.

6. I glue in the tips of all hackle feathers.

7. I whip finish thread heads with a double whip finish of 6-8 turns working back the hook shank and then 6-8 turns coming forward to the eye.

8. I compact all deer hair as much as possible using compacting pliers.

With bass flies, I will always opt for natural materials if I have a choice. Natural materials have several properties that make them more attractive to fish than synthetics. Someone might say, "But what about flash?" There is no natural substitute for flash and tinsel. If I need flash, I'm using synthetics to get it just like everyone else. But when choosing between craft fur, synthetic yak, and natural buck tail, I will go with natural buck tail for freshwater flies. Saltwater is a horse of a different color, because so many fish have teeth that will quickly reduce your flies to a bare hook if you tie with natural materials. Obviously, I use Enrico Puglisi fibers and Steve

Farrar's Flash Blends to create the Puglisi-style minnow flies. I also use compressed foam popper bodies instead of natural cork for my popper bodies. Natural materials have a more natural smell. They also will absorb natural smells from the water, mud, sand, etc. Synthetics smell like plastic. A wet buck tail streamer smells like a wet dog. That odor says "food" to a big ole bass! A guy recently asked me if I thought that a bait fish pattern that smelled like a wet rat instead of a fish would confuse a fish and cause him to be more hesitant. Fish's brains are not that complex. They see a bait fish and their brain says "food." They smell a wet mouse and their brain says "food." This is true even if it's the same lure sending both messages. The fish is twice as likely to bite, not less likely. It's not like someone handing you a cheeseburger that smells like watermelon and you think "Wait a minute! A cheeseburger shouldn't smell like a watermelon." You're a lot smarter than a fish. The fish sees cheeseburger, smells watermelon, and thinks "I better eat that!"

After tying your flies, leave them out to air cure for at least a full day before putting them in a fly box.  Then, give them a romp in the mud at the shore and rinse them out with pond or stream water before fishing them.  This will get a lot of the man-made and human scent off of them.

# *Chapter Six*

*My Magic Bag of Tricks*

Everyone suspects that anyone who is really successful at something has some secret formula, some magic bag of tricks, or some other esoteric knowledge that is the defining difference between their success and the mediocrity or failure of others. It's human nature. We all like to believe that we're just as good as the other guy, and when confronted with empirical evidence to the contrary, we try to explain it away. In reality, excellence is a combination of detailed study, a ton of trial and error, determination to keep at it for the long haul, and the courage to fail. These traits are invariably motivated by a passion for the process rather than the goal. People who love to swing clubs at tiny white balls while taking a walk in the woods will eventually get very good at golf. People who love to go fishing more than they care about what they catch will eventually become very good anglers. People who love to spend hours on end shooting baskets in an empty gym tend to become Michael Jordan. If you hate the process, you will not put in the hours and pursue the refinement of the process sufficiently to achieve excellence. The biggest secret to what makes one person a great fisherman and the rest just mediocre is that the excellent angler loves to cast, tie knots, play with tackle, hang out in the boat, wander up and down the banks of the river, and play with fish. He gets a kick out of catching a tiny Bluegill or a giant Tarpon. In fact, he gets a kick out of spending a whole day on the water in the blistering summer heat or a cold fall rain even if he catches nothing all day. He'd still rather do that than anything else. That person will become an excellent angler – sooner or later. Along the way, however, he will figure out a whole lot of what works best and what doesn't work so well. He'll also figure out a few things that are to be avoided like the plague. So, in a way, yes – the excellent angler will develop a magic bag of tricks. Let me show you what is inside mine.

We've already talked about *where* to fish for big bass, *when* to fish for big bass, and *what* to fish for big bass with.  Now we're going to discuss *how* to fish for trophy Bass.

## *Orientation to Shoreline*

The first thing that most anglers need to change about their fishing tactics in order to catch more quality Largemouth Bass is to *quit casting perpendicular to the bank*.  Whether they're out in a boat or standing on the shore, ninety five percent of the people I see fishing cast away from or directly toward the bank.  This is their first and most common mistake.  I cast parallel to or at an acute angle to the bank whether I'm in a boat, wading, or standing on the shore.  This has much less to do with imitating the bait the fish are feeding on than it does keeping your lure or fly in the sweet spot as long as possible.  Almost all structure runs roughly parallel to the nearest shoreline.  Only man-made structure or a fallen tree may run perpendicular to the

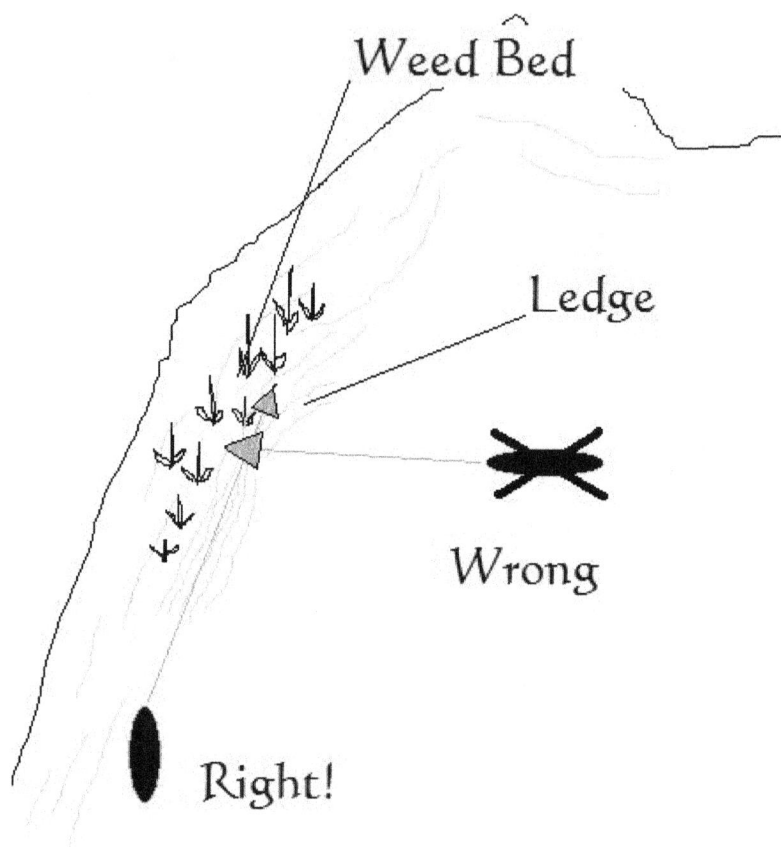

Figure 1: Above, you see a weed bed along the upper edge of a submerged ledge. Position the boat so that you can cast and retrieve parallel to these features instead of perpendicular to them.

shoreline. Weed beds, tree lines, and depth contours all mimic

the shoreline; not precisely, but pretty close to it. Furthermore,

bass are sensitive to light, temperature, and pressure. All of

that means they are very particular about depth. Look at a

nautical chart. The depth contours resemble the nearest

shoreline. If the bass are lying in three feet of water, why would

you cast to one foot of water and drag your fly through three

foot deep water and out into four, then five, and then six feet of

water trying to catch them? Cast as parallel to the bank as

possible along that 3 foot depth contour and retrieve your lure

or fly in 3 feet of water the whole time. You will never, ever

find bass holding in 2 through 12 feet of water near the same

spot at the same time. They will all be at about the same depth,

lying very near the bottom.

If the bass are cruising along the deep edge of a weed line,

why would you cast your fly to the shallow edge of the weed

line, then retrieve it across the weed bed and out beyond the

deep edge? Instead, cast parallel to the weed line...which is

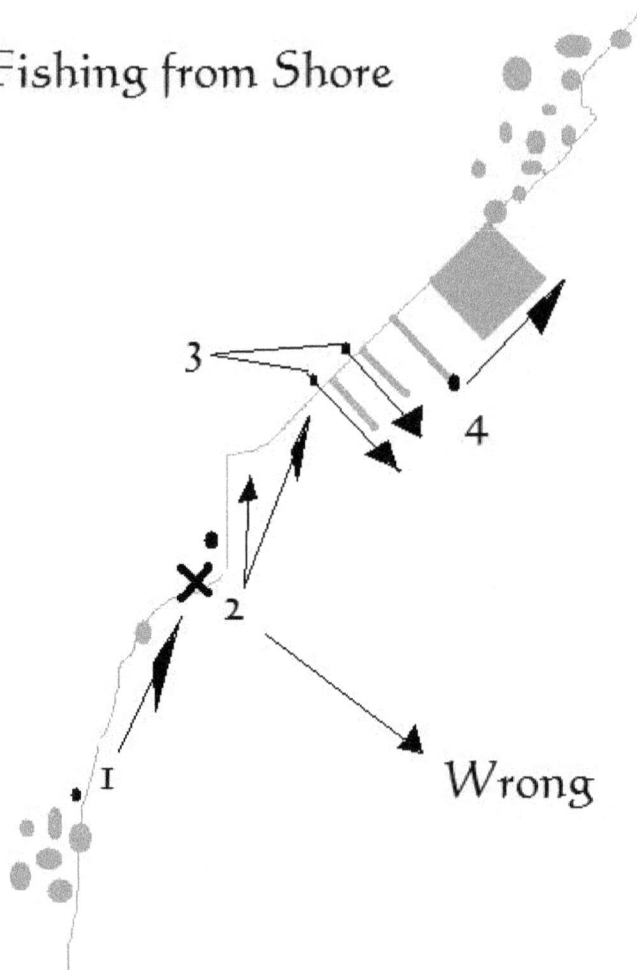

# Fishing from Shore

3

4

X
2

I

Wrong

Figure 2: Fishing from Shore: 1. Cast to point from bank; 2. Cover shallow water to dock from point; 3. Fish the docks; & 4. Fish shady front of boat house from adjacent dock. Don't stand on bank and cast straight out into deeper water without a darned good reason!

parallel to the shore...and keep your fly swimming right along the edge of the weed line throughout the retrieve.

*Casting as close to parallel to the shoreline as possible is the easiest thing you can change to increase the number of fish you catch when you go fishing.* Break the bad habit and replace it with a good one. You'll see a significant improvement in your fishing success. This applies to a lot more than lunker bass fishing!

## Sun and Shadows

Next, pay close attention to sunlight and shadows. In the warm part of the year, fish in the shadows. Remember, shadows work underwater, too. Submerged objects cast shadows underwater. Shaded water can often be a few degrees cooler than the adjacent sunny water. Sharp drop-offs and rises on the bottom create shadows underwater. Shade in the water is scarce from about ten thirty in the morning until about three in the afternoon. At this time, overhead cover provides most of the shade: docks, overhanging trees, deadfall, bridges, and so forth. A shaded bank in the afternoon will provide excellent relief to a big bass – and, coincidentally, to the bass fisherman.

In the cold part of the year, bass will seek warmer water. Fish the sunny banks and sun-exposures of structure. Grass and mud will hold warmth through the night. Bass will hunker down in the stuff. Sandy areas heat up quickly in direct sunlight, and the muddy areas and grass beds get too warm. Fish will spend their afternoons and evenings near light colored rock and sandy bottoms. But they will still prefer to stay out of direct sunlight when they're in shallow water. Bass do not like direct sunlight. They'd prefer to sit in the shade of a sunny dock than to sit along an exposed bank in direct sunlight. So you're still going to find the big fish in the smaller shadows on the sunny exposures of major features. Learn to make most of your casts into shadows and shady areas, because that is where you will find larger bass.

In both the Dog Days of Summer and the dead of Winter, you won't find as many large active bass in water less than four feet deep. This is particularly true in the heat of the day. Water temperature will rise into the eighties, water will shed oxygen, and bass become very uncomfortable and find it hard to breathe. So they go deeper. But you can still catch them. I focus on submerged structure that is in seven to fifteen feet of water, mostly closer to the ten foot range. Fish the bottom. This is a good time to add sonar to the equation, mostly to find the depth that most fish are holding in. Last week, I used my Humminbird fish finder to locate groups of fish while I paddled around a small lake. I found them in a hole that was about twenty feet deep, but most of them were only six to twelve feet deep. Using a sinking line and weighted flies, I used the count-down method to target five to ten feet deep and fished that area. I caught two Largemouth over four pounds in about forty-five minutes. Both fish struck the Clouser Minnow about ten feet deep. This is a good example of how to use sonar when fly-fishing.

Using sinking fly lines and large bait fish or crayfish patterns, I cast parallel to any structure. I fish slowly. Keep the rod and line in as straight of a line as possible to increase your sensitivity to a big bass inhaling your fly. Strip-setting the hook will be the only way to hook one this deep.

I look for the presence of shad and other minnows near the surface surrounding structure. This time of year, there are a lot of fry swimming in large schools in most area lakes. Regardless of what species these schools of small fish are, they are a key source of food for bass species. Big Largemouth feed on smaller Largemouth as soon as they leave the beds. Sometimes, a deep hole surrounded by relatively shallow water that lacks any definitive structure will hold a lot of shad and perhaps other predator fish, but Largemouth Bass do not like muddy, featureless bottoms. They are rarely present in such places, while Catfish, Hybrids, and White Bass are often lurking below the bait fish in spots like this. The deep edge of an aquatic grass bed adjacent to a significant ledge or drop-off or "shelf" will often produce in this way, and this is a prime spot to pick up Largemouth Bass. This is particularly true if the grass line or drop-off is oriented in such a way as to create shade along the bottom in the afternoon and evening sun. Find the structure and you'll find the Largemouth Bass. Generally, this reorientation of the Largemouth Bass to deeper water occurs in late June and persists until early October in most East Texas lakes.

You can still catch some in the shady shallows early in the morning and just before dark, but...generally speaking...daytime fishing has to account for these changes to be successful when hunting big Largemouth. So break out your sinking lines and heavier flies. If you like to fly-fish at night, and I don't, this is the time of year to do it. Fish top-water flies on floating lines near lighted docks for some shallow water action.

## Go Big or Go Home

I've already made this case a couple of times, but it cannot be over-stated. If you want to catch larger bass, fish with larger flies. That means you'll need heavier tackle.

Yes, you will catch fewer fish. But you will also catch bigger fish. Catching bigger bass is the whole point of this book. While there is no shortage of examples of exceptions to this rule of thumb, that's exactly what they are. If you want to increase your chances of catching really big fish, you need to ignore little fish and give the big ones every possible reason to take your fly.

## *Slow Down*

The run-and-gun approach that is so popular in conventional tackle fishing today isn't even a good strategy for conventional tackle fishing, but it is absolutely the wrong way to approach fly fishing for trophy quality fish. Run-and-gun is the idea that you bounce from spot to spot as quickly as possible, making a few casts at each location, and then moving on until you catch a fish. This approach only results in anglers catching the "low-hanging fruit" of what a fishery has to offer. Trophy bass are almost never "low-hanging fruit." This approach relies almost entirely on luck and lacks the finesse, stealth, and methodical approach necessary to locate and fool old fish with excellent instincts. You don't become consistent at catching superior fish by relying upon dumb luck. It has become popular due to the time constraints of most tournament formats. That's not because it is the most effective way to fish, but because it is the most effective way to fish for a few hours on one particular day. But even the good tournament anglers will only use this technique until they get bitten by a fish in the size class and species they are searching for on fisheries they don't fish regularly. When they do, they hunker down and try to catch the second and third ones with a methodical approach. It is usually these second and third quality fish from that same spot that will be the difference in winning or just participating in a tournament. In this day of instant gratification, quick fixes, fast food, and throwaway culture, most people mistake the way top pros fish their pre-selected spots until they find the fish they're looking for during tournaments and pre-fishing trips with the way they fish all of the time. The time constraint of a tournament is an artificial influence that is the result of the rules and serious tournament anglers are constantly moving from one fishery to another. If you remove the compressed time-frame and the requirement to move around like a gypsy from lake to lake, there is no reason to fish this way.

Fooling big old fish in shallow water requires patience. It requires stealth. It requires some thought. And it requires a bit of tenacity. If you see fifty yards of excellent shoreline cover in the afternoon shade, you don't zoom right up to it in a motorboat and wash the whole shoreline with a big wake, then drop a trolling motor and cruise down the shore banging the bank every fifty feet and call it quits if you don't get lucky. And that's the way eighty percent of folks fish nowadays.

Instead, slow way down at least a hundred and fifty yards from your destination. Drop that trolling motor gently and sit there until your own wake is gone. Now troll in at low speed until you're in casting range. Cut the motor. Make several casts no more than a few feet apart to cover the entire shoreline thoroughly. When you've covered what you can reach or the boat drifts out of position, turn the trolling motor on low and ease along until you get to the spot you like. Set yourself up to where the wind helps position your boat if at all possible, instead of having to use the motor to fight against wind or current. While we're on a high probability spot, we avoid opening and closing hatches on the boat, dropping things on the deck, or any loud noises. Put the boat in a position that allows you to cast and retrieve along the cover instead of perpendicular to it.  Work from one end toward the other end, casting to new water as you move.  Do not bother to cast back where the boat has been.

A big bass will not move far to take a fly very often.  Set the boat at your maximum effective casting range (effective means you can throw a fly into a trash can from that distance) and retrieve back only about twenty feet of line before picking it up to re-cast.  Only use a trolling motor or paddle as much as necessary to keep the boat where you want it.  Feel free to ease an anchor over the side and gently drop it to the bottom in order to hold a spot for awhile, but remember to put out plenty of anchor line (a thirty degree angle or less between boat and anchor).  That means you'll need to be upwind/upstream of where you want the boat to be by that length of rope.  If you drop an anchor, make a loud noise, etc., you may want to sit quietly for a few minutes before casting.  I almost always pause for a drink or a smoke or even a snack when I get my boat set in position to fish a spot. Fish have a conscious awareness (memory) of about five minutes, max. Once your boat has been sitting quietly in place for a few minutes, it is a natural part of the fish's environment. The shadow of the boat, any reflections or noises you've made, etc. aren't scary anymore. The fish begin to relax and return to business as usual. Bang a paddle against the hull or drop a fishing rod or tackle box, and you're back to the waiting game again. Stillness is your best camouflage from fish. That means the lack of both motion and noise.

As you see, my approach to fishing a spot is slow, methodical, and patient. If I think top-water flies are going to work, I'll fish the whole spot with a top-water fly. It will cover every square foot or two of the area about twenty feet at a time. If that didn't work, I'm not finished. You've heard the old saying, "Never leave fish to find fish," right? Well, I never leave a "fishy spot" to find fish until I've fished it at least two different ways.

Next, I'm going to fish something bigger, smaller, or deeper. If conditions have changed, I may change colors or weight of a fly. I'll repeat the entire process. If I still haven't caught a fish, I will pick up another rod or re-rig and try something else. I take a break now and then to let the fish forget I'm there casting flies in their vicinity. This process will take at least an hour – to fish fifty to a hundred yards of prime linear structure. But experience has taught me that if I do it this way, I can count on catching at least one bass over twenty inches long every other hour that I fish. Sometimes, I'll catch three to five in one spot like this. And the pace is very relaxing.

While you're fishing at this sort of pace, you have plenty of time to notice the little things. A quivering tuft of weeds or emergent branch that is a giveaway that a big fish lurks just below, a school of bait that swims in from behind me, the Great Blue Heron just caught his second Bluegill a couple hundred yards back up the way I came, the clouds are thickening and the breeze has picked up and changed directions – all of these things provide me with clues about what to do or not to do. *If you don't notice these things very often, slow down!* You're fishing way too fast to be the master of your own destiny. You're relying on blind luck.

By the way, when you fish at a slower, relaxed, and observant pace, you will come to realize just how little of a body of water you need to have a great time and catch huge bass! Eventually, you'll look at a big farm pond and think to yourself, "It would take me all day to fish this thing." Suddenly, those big tourist lakes lose some of their appeal.

## Go Deep!

Don't be afraid to fish deep with a fly rod. Fly-fishing is quite effective down to about twenty feet deep with the right tackle. Most East Texas lakes are always holding a good number of Largemouth over twenty inches in water less than twenty feet deep. A lot of the year, you can catch temperate bass in water less than twenty feet deep. Big flies with a bit of weight on them and a good sinking line on a fairly fast action rod will do the trick. Retrieve most of the line, roll cast the fly to the surface, and immediately pick it up and re-cast it. Count it down. Retrieve it again. In late Summer and in the dead of Winter, you will have to fish deeper to consistently find quality fish. In my experience on East Texas lakes, that means ten to twenty feet. But here's the key: eighty percent of all Largemouth Bass are within a foot of the bottom no matter where they are. The bigger the fish, the more reliable that behavioral pattern becomes. You'll catch Largemouth Bass in the ten to fifteen inch range suspending, ganged up on pods of shad, or just transiting around the lake. Once they're bigger than about fifteen inches, they stop doing this. For starters, there aren't as many fish over fifteen inches and fish tend to group with fish of similar size to keep from being eaten by bigger fish. Really big bass become apex predators, masters of their own domains. They become more solitary and are almost never found in groups of more than three fish. Temperate Bass will suspend at mid and shallow depths with great frequency and exhibit schooling behavior, but Largemouth Bass do not.

## *Roll, Baby Roll!*

Learn to roll cast. In fact, learn some single-handed Spey casting. Get *really good* at roll casting! Learn to make side-arm casts from a water anchor, airborne roll casts (no water anchor), and at least the single and double Spey. Fishing that water under the overhanging branches, under the docks, and under the low bridges will produce a lot of your biggest bass. Roll casting is extremely accurate, surprisingly stealthy (seems counter-intuitive to people, but makes perfect sense to fish), and amazingly impervious to wind. But it also allows you to put flies in very tight spaces – *lunker Largemouth Bass live most of their lives in very tight places.* The importance of good roll casting for the bass and trout angler is hard to over-state, and it is one of the main reasons that I don't like stiff fly rods. Stiff rods simply do not roll cast worth a darn.

## *Strippers versus Pole Dancers*

You want to become a master stripper and avoid pole dancing at all cost. Learn and practice several different retrieves using your line hand. Sometimes, big fish are triggered by a fast-moving fly, but rarely. Most of the time, big bass are going to take the biggest meal they can catch with a little bit of effort. Learn to move a fly delicately without covering much water (ie. without retrieving much line). This is very seductive to all sunfish species, including Largemouth Bass. Learn to make poppers pop and divers dive with short, quick strips that allow your fly to remain in the zone longer through more repetitions.  But also learn the figure eight retrieve, which produces a slow, steady swimming pace.  And learn to retrieve very long, slow strips that keep a fly down near the bottom when fishing a full sinking line.  Learn to keep your rod pointed at the water parallel to the fly line.  Your rod tip should be hovering just over or right on the water's surface when fishing with a floating line, and your rod tip will often need to be underwater when fishing with sinking lines.  This will help you detect even the most subtle takes of a big ole bass that inhales your fly from the side or while moving toward you (which they do quite frequently).

*When you detect a take, do not...I'll say it again...do not move your fly rod!*  Dispense of any notion you may have of a big, rod-bending hook set on that lunker bass.  That's for guys fishing with heavy bait or spin-casting tackle.  Instead, *strip*...long, hard, and fast.  Hold on to the fly line and don't let line slip for the first second or two, at least.  I try to hold them for at least three seconds.  Now you think about putting the fight into the rod.  But that does not mean to raise your rod tip!

If you're fishing in submerged cover that isn't visible at the

surface, raise your rod to a forty-five degree angle (and no

more).  If you're fishing in emergent vegetation, this fish is

already diving and rooting through the weed stalks, branches,

etc.  Keep your rod tip down...underwater...and bend the rod to

the side away from the fish at a forty-five degree angle.  You

don't want to try and pull the fish *up* through the weeds or Lily

Pads.  You want to pull him *out* of them.  The shortest distance

between two points is a straight line.  Apply pressure that will

coax the fish to the outer edge of the weeds, or to a large hole

in the weeds.  If the fish struck under or at the edge of a dock,

keep the rod tip down. Pull him *away* from the structure.

Mostly, you're trying to stay connected and keep moderate

pressure on the fish using the butt section of your rod.  The

thickest section of your rod just above the grip is the only piece

of the fly rod that will wear a good fish out or allow you to guide

the direction a fish is swimming.  You must keep the rod at

forty-five degrees or less orientation to an imaginary line between you and the fish in order to engage the fish with this part of the fly rod. Don't try to force the fish to go where you want him to. Your attitude should be one of a determined negotiator. Think of it like you've hooked your wife in the mouth to keep her from running off a cliff. You're going to have to answer for this later! Be firm, but empathetic. Try to save her life without pissing her off any worse than she already is.

If you cannot keep the line from slipping, let just as much slip as necessary…slowly, in a controlled manner. Don't let go! And whatever you do, do not try to "put the fish on the reel" by releasing the line and quickly reeling up the excess! This is a critical error that will cost you almost any fish truly worthy of a good reel's drag. If that fish needs to be on the reel, he'll get there whether you want him to or not. Resist with steady, but pliable pressure. That's precisely what the drag on your reel will do anyway. Yes, you might lose a few fish getting the hang of playing them by hand. Trust me, it's worth losing a few to get the hang of it so that you don't lose them all.  If you lose

pressure on that fish, he will spit the hook out.  I guarantee you

that.  Your only chance is to maintain the bend in the rod now.

If you try to set the hook by raising the rod tip, all of this is

for naught.  You'll never be able to set a hook deeply and

quickly enough to catch trophy size Largemouth, Stripers, or

Hybrid if you try to set the hook with the rod tip.  That works on

bream, trout, and crappie.  You have to punch through some

serious cartilage as often as not to hook a big bass!  Sharp hooks

and a strip set are the keys to success.  One of the best known

Largemouth Bass fly-fishing guides in this part of the country,

who has made his reputation putting fly anglers on trophy bass

at Lake Fork, has written and taught about this extensively.

He's often said that the first thing he does with all of his new

clients is to have them practice a strip set until they've got the

"trout set" out of their system.  Then they go fishing.

## *Give Up to Win*

Inevitably, a big fish will eventually wrap your line around a tree stump, limb, or dock piling. If you hook enough of them, that's bound to happen. When it does, I hope you remember what I'm about to tell you. I saw someone do it once. A few months later, I hooked the largest Rainbow Trout of my life near a deadfall in a river on a nymph. This Steelhead sized Rainbow went right back where it came from under the root wad, and there was nothing my five weight fly rod and 5X tippet were going to do to stop her. She wrapped me up in the root wad. Then I remembered what I saw my friend do in Colorado in a similar situation with a big Brown trout. I released the pressure, created a bit of slack, and waited.

A couple was paddling by and stopped. The lady asked, "Are you hung up?"

"I've got a big Rainbow on, but she wrapped me in the root wad. I'm just going to wait and see if she works herself out," I explained.

217

You see, that fish didn't just hang *me* up. She hung *both of us* up. And the way I figured it, this was her natural environment. She was far more likely to free herself than I was to free us. So I waited. Sure, she might spit the hook, but she might *not*. One thing was sure though: she wasn't going to tolerate that situation for long!

Out she came! I was still hooked up. Now she was in open water. I followed her downstream away from the log. Then I put the fight to her. She came to hand after several minutes, and I'll bet she was every bit of seven pounds and the best part of thirty inches long. I looked up to see the couple in the kayaks and about three more guys who had floated down during the fight all back-paddling to hold their position near me.

"That was amazing!" the woman exclaimed.

"That's the biggest trout I've ever seen caught in this river," one of the older men said.

By the time I returned to the camp we were all staying at downstream a few hours later, word had spread. Everyone wanted to know about my huge Rainbow. I learned a valuable lesson about working with nature instead of against her that day. I also learned something about human nature. Most of the time when you're struggling with someone and it comes to a stand-off, you'll get a much better outcome if you let people think the solution was their idea. They probably don't like being stuck any more than you do.

Since then, I've tried this four times. Three times, I ended up landing the fish. Once, it spit the hook and left me standing there snagged. The way I see it, that figures out to 4 out of 5 times. That's an 800 batting average in baseball. Do you know anyone with an 800 batting average in baseball? I'll take those odds!

When that big fish wraps you up on something, try to give it enough slack to work itself free. Sit there and wait. It takes anywhere from several seconds to a couple of minutes. More often than not, the fish will swim free and still be hooked – if

you react quickly enough when the line comes free. So don't go

to sleep!

## *Check Your Leader*

We spend an inordinate amount of money on our rods,

reels, and fly lines. Yet...even if you fish with inexpensive

tackle...the portion of your rig that is going to fail nine times out

of ten is your leader, tippet, or hook. This is as sure as gravity.

You should check your leader and fly so frequently that your

fishing buddies will think you suffer from Obsessive-Compulsive

Disorder. When you're fishing for trophy fish, you cannot afford

to stick a fish with a wind knot in your leader. You cannot

afford to make "one more cast" with a frayed piece of tippet

above your fly. You cannot afford to discover your hook point

wasn't sharp enough, or the hook was bent, when you miss the

hook set. Chances to catch trophy fish just don't come along

that often. If you snag a fly or errantly cast it against a hard

object, you need to check your terminal tackle and correct

anything that isn't perfect. Hook points should bite into your fingernail with the least pressure. If it doesn't, hit it with a hook sharpener before continuing to fish. Discoloration in tippet or leader indicates a stressed portion. Cut it off above the discoloration and re-rig. Similarly, a piece of leader or tippet that has been damaged by external abrasion will turn whitish. It will usually kink a bit, but not always. Cut off above the damage and re-rig immediately. Wind knots are sure to cut your line under heavy stress. Checking my terminal tackle and re-rigging to make corrections is how I spend most of those short breaks in casting I mentioned earlier. A few days ago, I realized the hook shank on my fly was broken smooth in half while inspecting it during a smoke break after releasing a pretty good bass after a hard fight in the weeds. The fly still looked perfect, but when I grabbed it to check the hook point and knot, it wiggled in the middle like an articulated fly. It wasn't an articulated fly. If you want to collect memories of big fish landed instead of stories about the ones that got away, you should do the same.

## *Cadence is King*

I've had the privilege of fishing with a lot of great fly anglers over the years. Without exception, they have all been very particular about the cadence with which they retrieve a fly. It varies from species to species, and by time and place; but finding the right rhythm and speed with which to retrieve a fly is a critical element of triggering strikes.

Modern lure companies have figured this out, and spend a lot of time and resources in research and development working on the cadence of crank baits, spinner baits, chatter baits, and so forth. Many top professional bass anglers customize and "fine tune" their top quality lures in the boat to make adjustments to the cadence of the lure. Twist a blade or lip, swap the hooks for heavier or lighter ones, or bend the arm on a spinner bait – are all examples of the tinkering with pliers that goes on to get just the right cadence with conventional tackle. In fly-fishing, good fly design and construction plays a smaller

John Holsten is a fly-fishing guide from Cotter, Arkansas, who spends most of his time helping people catch trout. In his free time, he puts on a Hawaiian shirt and goes bass fishing. (Image: John Holsten, 2014.)

role.  Primarily, it's what the angler does with the line in his off-hand that will determine the cadence of a fly.

Personally, I find that the common twitch-twitch-twitch-pause, twitch-twitch-twitch-pause is the most universally attractive to predator fish.  One second per twitch is too slow.  Two or three twitches per second followed by a half second pause is usually about right.  This is my starting point for finding the right cadence in each particular time and place.  Some fairly new research in this area has been helpful.  Many crank bait manufacturers now include weighted rattles in their lures to create more cadence.  They've discovered...through much trial and error...that in brighter light and clearer water, fish are more likely to strike when you present to them with a faster cadence, while in lower light and murkier water the fish are more likely to strike with a slower cadence.  The same thing is basically true with cold or warm water temperatures.  You need to slow down in cold water, because the fish's metabolism is slower.  They simply won't be able to expend a lot of energy chasing a fast-moving fly.  If the water temperature hits eighty degrees, you also have to slow down.  The water is releasing dissolved oxygen, and fish will get "winded" very quickly if they exert a lot of energy.  When the water temperature is in the low to mid seventies, that's when your cadence should be the quickest.

Sometimes, experimentation will tell you that two twitches and a pause works better than three.  Sometimes, I've gotten best results with up to five twitches before the pause.  In yet other scenarios, I've found out that the fish will bite reliably during a long pause of several seconds in duration when using flies that float or suspend well.  In fact, big Largemouth Bass will often take a top-water fly that has been sitting motionless on the water for as much as three minutes.  There's nothing wrong at all with casting a deer hair popper or diver into a hole in the Lily Pads and just letting it sit there for awhile as if you were fishing live bait under a bobber.  You may twitch it ever so slightly once or twice without actually dragging the fly across the surface – just to give it some life-like movement.  Frogs often sit on the surface relatively motionless, but they'll breathe, twitch a leg, etc. at least once a minute or so. Sometimes, a big bass will inhale such a presentation. I've had it happen several times when I wasn't expecting it. The fly suddenly disappears from the surface in a little swirl that you'll miss if you blink. At least three times that I can recall, I've set the hook when I didn't see my fly where I expected to after fiddling with my slack line, drag, a cigarette, or a bottle of water and actually hooked a very nice bass. You see, a big bass will approach slowly from underneath. If he can get within range without spooking his prey, he'll suddenly flare his gills and open his massive mouth, inhaling a huge amount of water that will suck his unsuspecting prey right in. If you can see your fly in or on the water and it disappears, set the hook! Sometimes, it might just be a shadow or slight change in the fly's depth. But sometimes, it will be that trophy Bucketmouth! A bass large enough to inhale your fly without you feeling it is definitely a prize fish. Don't sit there and wonder if it was or wasn't. Find out!

## *Fish It Out*

When you make a casting error and your fly lands on the bank, a dock, in a bush, or what not, don't give up and start thinking about how to get your fly back for the next cast. There are several reasons why you still need to be thinking about presentation. We call this "fishing it out." It's also true about missed strikes. Fish them out. The first Tarpon I ever landed was a fish that hit my fly after a badly mangled tailing loop that landed well short of where I had seen the fish roll on the surface. I let the fly and line settle for a bit, then slowly and smoothly took up the slack to straighten out the line. On the first strip, the fish hit. I got the hook into him. The experts say that if you can stay hooked to a tarpon for about fifteen seconds, you've got a good chance of landing them. In my limited experience, this seems pretty true. I've never lost one much further than that into the fight. The first one I jumped may have gone thirty seconds, but I totally screwed up the fight on that one when it turned and rushed the boat. Feeling the slack, I lifted the rod tip. You can't do that with Tarpon. You have to take up the slack as quickly as possible without raising the rod tip. That means you get off the reel and strip in the slack line, allowing it to pile up at your feet again. The fish will take that line again. You just have to keep from getting tangled up in it, because when he takes the line it happens so fast that you don't have but a split-second to react. Many Tarpon fishermen have ended up in the ocean with fly line wrapped around their ankle. Not good! It can be very dangerous. But raising the rod tip will inevitably allow the fish to spit the fly out. This is largely due to the shape of their mouth and the fact that hooks rarely penetrate the thick cartilage plates that form their mouths until the fish has pulled long enough against your resistance to embed the hook. Make a mistake with a hundred pound or bigger silver torpedo on your line, and that fish will make you regret it. An adult tarpon is often older than the angler who hooks him. There's a very good chance that this ain't his first rodeo! But the first one I actually landed came after a terribly errant cast.

If your fly lands in a bush, on top of some floating vegetation, across a limb, or what have you, drag the fly smoothly and very slowly until it clears the obstacle and plops gently into the water. Most of the time, the fly will be near the spot you were casting to anyway. Now fish the fly as usual. The fly is far more likely to slip through or over the obstacle without snagging if you use slow, delicate, smooth retrieval of the fly line. If you jerk it, twitch it, etcetera, you are far more likely to tangle it in a bush or weeds, or snag it on a dock or tree branch. This is especially true with flies with weed guards. Dave Whitlock taught me this trick many years ago using a fly with no weed guard by casting it into a shoreline bush intentionally several times, and I have caught many good fish when that fly finally plops lightly into the water since then.

Often times, the bass you suspected was there when you made the cast has become curious by the slight movement of the bushes, or the vibration of your fly scooting along the dock. Many times, she can see the shadow and motion. To her, it looks like food. She was laying there waiting to ambush something just like this. This is especially true with Lily Pads. Slowly and gently skitter that fly along the Lily Pads until it plops into the water right next to one. My personal best Largemouth Bass was caught exactly this way. The fly slipped off the edge of a pad at least a yard back into the weed bed into a hole about eighteen inches in diameter. The weeds moved and the fly disappeared. I set the hook and the Lily Pads erupted with commotion. Fish on! I buried my rod tip underwater and leaned back into the butt section of the rod as I refused to give her line, pressuring her toward the edge of the weeds – across the bow of my kayak. She swam clear and brought about a dozen Lily Pad plants with her. I gave her some line and she crossed into open water. Executing a reversal of side pressure and bringing the rod to the other side of the boat, I encouraged her to free herself of the ten pound knot of weeds. Now it was just the two of us in open water. She was gorgeous and huge! I landed that fish on twelve pound test, and that's about what she weighed.  Measuring her against the ruler on my paddle,

she was twenty-eight inches long.

So when you make an errant cast, go ahead and fish it out.

Don't pick up the fly just because you missed.  When you cast

into bushes and such, stop.  Take a breath.  Retrieve the fly

slowly and smoothly to try and free it from the obstacle.

Sometimes, this is the most convincing presentation of all.

Likewise, I've caught many bigger fish after missing a strike

from a smaller fish.  Fish are competitive.  The bigger they are,

the more competitive they become.  Nothing improves your

odds of getting fish to bite like more fish in the vicinity, and

that's not just because of the numbers.  A hungry fish doesn't

want to miss out on a good meal.  If he fools around for long,

that other fish might eat it first.  Every sentient being is

motivated by a combination of hope of gain and fear of loss.

Creatures are far more likely to act when *both* are compelling

arguments at the same time.  This works at a very instinctive

level in all of us critters, whether we are able to think it through rationally or not. It's the foundation of our survival instincts. But we tend to revel in the failure to hook that first fish and react to that, thereby giving up on the reality that it is actually more likely for the next few seconds that another fish will take our fly. If we allow ourselves to become distracted, we shout a choice word or phrase, and we stop fishing – even for a second or three – we cancel out the advantage we just gained. *Fish it out!*

## Get a Net

Most of my life, I have fished without the aid of a landing net. It's just how I "grew up" fishing, and I never really saw the need for them. A few years ago, my boat sponsor asked me to fish the Jacksonville Kayak Fishing Classic, the world's largest kayak fishing tournament (and one of the biggest amateur fishing tournaments in the world). This is an in-shore saltwater fishing tourney based in Jacksonville, Florida, and we would be fishing for Sea Trout, Redfish, and Flounder. The biggest fish in each category won a substantial prize package worth thousands of dollars, and the biggest combination of all three fish won the overall championship.

About half way through the morning, I landed the biggest Flounder I had ever seen live and in person. I got it into the boat without a net or my Fish Grip, but it was flopping around mercilessly – as Flounder usually do. I got the fish on the measuring tape in the deck of my kayak and saw that it was roughly twenty-seven inches long. Then I realized I didn't have my camera turned on.'I couldn't do it with one hand. I tried a couple of times to no avail. As soon as I took my other hand off the fish, it flopped out of the boat. It was still hooked! (take a hint from that, too) But that didn't last for long. The fish flopped and turned and spit the hook out of its mouth sitting right beside my boat on the surface. It actually just slowly drifted down out of sight below the surface. It took about three seconds for it to disappear. Immediately, I thought to myself, "A twenty dollar net would have saved that fish and probably won you over a thousand dollars." You see, the day before I had almost stopped to buy a net, but I talked myself out of it. Well, the Flounder that took first was twenty six inches long. I had it beaten if I could have controlled that fish long enough to get the photo. To save twenty bucks, I had cost myself more than a thousand dollars. The next day, I went to the sporting goods store and bought a high quality folding and telescoping fishing net. It has been in my boat ever since, and I often carry it when fishing from the bank. It has landed dozens of fish over ten pounds since.

In fact, every good fish I bring to the boat gets netted nowadays. I no longer touch the fish with my hands. I bring them into the boat in the net, immediately lock the Fish Grip on their lower lip, then I remove the hook. I measure them using the ruler on the shaft of my paddle and then slide them over the side of the boat for revival with the Fish Grip. When they seem ready to go, I release the jaws of the Fish Grip and they swim away. Now and then, I'll snap a quick picture. But I don't do that very often because I believe the fish should not be out of the water any longer than I can comfortably hold my breath without stress. I learned that from fisheries biologists. That's how I time it, too. When I lift the net out of the water, I hold my breath. When I start feeling the urge to breathe, it's time for the fish to go back into the water. I'd much rather provide you with the opportunity to catch the fish than to provide you with a picture of me catching the fish via the Internet. But since I bought my net, I haven't lost a quality fish at the boat or bank.

## *Speaking of Competition*

I don't compete for fishing spots. If you want it, you can have it. I know plenty more spots where I am just as likely to catch just as many fish that are just as big. If I don't want to go to a different spot right now, I'll hang back well beyond the range where you will even notice me and wait. Most folks nowadays don't fish a spot for very long. And I am notorious for catching good fish behind other anglers. If you ever fish a stream with me, you'll probably find that I tell you to take the lead. I'll follow along a couple of minutes behind you. Fish have a very short window of consciousness.  Remember?  I don't like being "pushed" from behind, but I don't mind fishing the water you were fishing a few minutes ago at all.  It'll take me most of the time that it takes the fish to forget the other guy was there just to get into position.  Then I let things settle for a few minutes.  Then I catch the fish he missed.  Sometimes, I'll catch the ones he caught.  This applies to shore and pier fishing, wading, and fishing from boats in lakes, rivers, or the ocean.

## *What You See is What You Get*

Don't get me wrong, I have taught blind people to fly-fish with the aid of someone who can see.  But I think it would be extremely difficult for a blind person to assist another blind person, or for a blind person to fly-fish alone.  I'm not saying that it couldn't be done, but I would marvel at the accomplishment.  The better your vision is, the more of an advantage you have in fly-fishing.

There are several reasons why you should spare no expense to protect and enhance your vision when fly-fishing.  First, you want to protect your eyes from flying debris, waterborne contaminants, and an errant fly. Second, you will be enduring a lot of ultra-violet light exposure. UV rays are a primary cause of cataracts and glaucoma. Third, glare will give you a raging headache that will drive anyone to quit fishing. Fourth, a great pair of polarized sunglasses in the right darkness and tint for the conditions you're fishing in can greatly enhance your visual perception. This includes the ability to see several feet to several yards below the water's surface, depending on ambient light and water turbidity. On a bright day on the open ocean, it is not uncommon to be able to see fish near the boat as much as fifty feet below the surface. Sight-casting to schooling Dorado in four hundred feet of water was one of the coolest experiences of my fishing life. None of those fish were hooked less than thirty feet deep, and we caught five in rapid succession using jigging spoons on spinning rods. Without good polarized glasses, none of us could have seen those fish.

When bass fishing, I don't usually sight-cast to fish I can see. If you can see a Largemouth Bass, it can see you, too. If a Largemouth Bass knows you're there, it isn't going to eat anything. Period. End of discussion. This is not true of most other bass species, nor is it true of a whole lot of non-bass species. But it is definitely true of big Largemouth Bass! But that doesn't mean that the ability to see the surface, surroundings, and below the surface doesn't help me catch more big Largemouth Bass. The ability to watch the smaller fish in an area gives me good clues to where the big one might be. The ability to detect shadows and bright areas underwater tells me a lot about where to cast. And the ability to see the fish I've hooked already aids me greatly in playing the fish successfully to hand. Glare wipes out a lot of detail in your field of vision. Things like turtles, frogs, Dragonflies, snakes, and other small and subtle movements in the vicinity give me many clues about where the big bass are and what they're doing. Disturbed silt clouds in the water tell me big fish are active nearby – perhaps I just bumped one out of hiding. That tells me I'm too close.

238

While playing a fish, I may spy a submerged log in the vicinity. I'll want to try and maneuver the fish away from that. I can see trot lines and other hazards much more clearly. I could go on and on. The moral of the story is simple: get yourself a couple of pairs of the best polarized sunglasses you can afford and wear them at all times on the water.

Another useful item for motor boat anglers is a good pair of wide field binoculars with polarized lenses and at least four power magnification. You can sit in one spot and survey everything within line of sight for feeding birds, surface activity, and to get a better idea of what other boaters are doing. Simply put, good binoculars will improve your situational awareness by extending the range of your vision out in all directions. That can save you a lot of time and fuel.

## X Marks the Spot

Modern real-time GPS navigation devices coupled with high quality navigational and fishing chart software greatly enhances your ability to fish submerged structure with precision. I use

Navionics Marine & Lakes USA on a smart phone when I'm in my kayak. Humminbird makes a wide variety of great electronics consoles that work very well with Navionics+ software cards for different sizes and types of boats. These units incorporate sonar, which can be useful in deep water. I think sonar is more valuable for fly-fishing for temperate bass than I do for Largemouth Bass. Largemouth Bass tend to come shallow to feed. Most of their deep water haunts are sanctuary, or resting, locations. They're not actually very active when they're holding near the bottom in water more than twenty feet deep. We can't reach them deeper than about twenty feet with fly tackle, anyway. So I tend to ignore deep water bass in spite of all of the hoopla about fishing deep for lunker Largemouth nowadays. As a fly-fisherman, it's just not relevant. Even fishing conventional tackle, it's a pretty low percentage game in East Texas most of the year. Yes, the guy who brings in the biggest bass in the tournament may have caught that thirteen pound fish in thirty-five feet of water, but the guy who wins the tournament caught five eight pound fish in fifteen feet of water.

I've seen it happen over and over again. All of this talk about water depth changes when you start going North, but in East Texas our lakes are fairly shallow. Water that is too deep to fly-fish effectively is mostly sanctuary habitat for big Largemouth Bass. Getting them to bite while they're resting is not the high-probability approach to fishing. We want to find them actively feeding. Most of the time, big Largemouth feed in water that is less than twenty feet deep in East Texas.

On the other hand, that real-time geo-located Navionics map comes in very handy! I can use it to position my boat to within one foot of resolution over any sort of submerged structure. It takes the guessing out of the equation. I use it a lot. I use it to educate myself about fisheries I'm not all that familiar with. I use it to plan fishing trips. And I use it to position my boat while fishing. I know that it has put more and bigger fish in my boat several times, and it has allowed me to fish unfamiliar waters with greater confidence and precision.

## *The Waiting Game*

I told you earlier that we'd talk more about the value of suspending flies in the water column as a powerful presentation for Largemouth Bass.  Let me explain that in detail now.

Awhile back, I wrote about letting a surface fly sit still – and maybe just twitching it ever so slightly once a minute or so.  Big bass will often take that when no other surface presentation works.

Similarly, bait fish that suddenly stop and wait, suspended below the surface – not moving – are exceptionally life-like.  Nobody's lures stop and just hang there in the water like a real fish.  They either begin to float to the surface or sink.  But real fish, by using their air bladder, can just hover motionless in place.

We all know the key is a "life-like" presentation.  What we often overlook is that wild critters spend a good bit of their time sitting still.  This includes the littler fish that big predator fish feed upon.  We're all familiar with fishermen saying, "They were

242

taking it on the drop," or "they took it on the pause." It makes

hooking fish efficiently a bit trickier, because the average angler

doesn't detect that take until he or she moves the lure or fly

again. Many times, the fish are already spitting it out by the

time we notice. I've already told you the best way to combat

that is to set the hook if you lose sight of the fly. What about

when you can't see the fly? Well, that's why they call it fishing

instead of catching! The changes in line tension, subtle

movement of the line where it disappears into the water, or

that sideways drift of just an inch or so can be very hard to

detect. It takes great situational awareness and focus. We all

miss some. Most of us miss most of them.

If you can't see the fly, watch the end of the fly line on a

floating line or the line you can see just outside the rod tip on a

sinking line. Any change in that portion of the fly line that you

did not cause is likely to be a fish at the other end. A strip-set

will let you know, one way or the other. If a big bass inhales

your fly from the side, the leader will move in that direction.

243

This is often subtle at the tip of a floating line, and sometimes undetectable with a sinking line if there is any slack in it at all. This is one reason why I like to use long, slow retrieves with only minimal pauses when fishing deep. It keeps the slack out of the line, and that makes strike detection easier. On a floating or intermediate sinking line that isn't too deep, you can often see the end of the fly line – either on the surface or just below. If that tip moves sideways, set the hook! In both cases, if there is an increase in line tension (or that bit of slack disappears) when you're holding still, set the hook! The worst thing that happens with a good strip-set is that you move the fly a foot or two pretty quickly. If you try to set with the rod tip, you'll pull the fly out of the water. You may even hit yourself in the chest or face with it. See? There's another compelling reason to use a strip-set instead of tip-set.

When I can see my flies below the surface, I like to fish Wool Head Muddlers and Puglisi Minnows. The Wool Head Muddler takes a great weed guard. So I'll fish with it in the thick stuff. If there's open water to be fished, I'll use Puglisi Minnows because they're naturally more neutrally buoyant. Stop stripping a well-tied EP Minnow and it just sits there, neither sinking nor rising toward the surface. It will sink very slowly – almost too slowly to see – perhaps an inch every two to five seconds. That's mostly due to the weight of the hook. If you have Largemouth Bass lurking about waiting for a shad or sunfish to swim by carelessly, you can get a ton of mileage out of pausing a suspending bait fish fly in the danger zone. Keeping the fly in the strike zone as much as possible is the big goal here anyway. This is true whether the fly is moving or not. If you can let it sit still, that's so much the better. Now, of course, you'll want to twitch it a little bit now and then to attract attention. But keep it in that kill zone for as long as possible without re-casting. We do this a lot when fishing dock lights at night for Snook in Florida. You can see everything. You cast the fly up under the edge of the dock or as close to it as possible. If nothing moves, you twitch it and wait. Wait some more. Then twitch it again. The fly hasn't moved six inches

245

from where it landed.  Play this game long enough and that big old Snook laying back in the shadows under the dock will streak out and grab it.  Game on!  Largemouth Bass and Snook are very similar in their behaviors and temperaments.  So I started using this technique on Largemouth Bass, too.  It works just as well. In fact, I'd love to try some night fishing on Texas lakes with dock and bridge lights and such to see how it works in exactly the same scenario.

The times and places where you'll find this most useful in East Texas when fishing for Largemouth Bass are during the spawning season of Spring  and immediately following end of spawning season in June (maybe into early July some years).  If you throw a suspending bait fish fly that looks like a big Bluegill into the bass beds, those big ole bass are going to tear it up! They will not tolerate the Bluegills coming in there and eating their babies.  Keep it right on the bed and twitch it ever so slightly now and then.  After the bass have spawned out and the water starts to get hot, some big bass will hang in deeper water just on the edge of the bream beds. They'll pick off strays and stragglers from the hordes of little bream that are hanging around the beds. This is another great place to snag a pretty wary bass by pausing that suspending bait fish fly in front of their face. Don't be afraid of slow retrieves. Don't be afraid of letting that fish get a good look at your fly. In fact, be persistent and try to piss him off with it if you know where he's at. If you see the fly disappear, set the hook! Any change in tension, including the unexplained appearance of slack, should cause you to set the hook. Sideways motion – set the hook. A flash of white in the vicinity of your fly - set the hook!

Most flies that you're going to bounce along the bottom should be fished pretty slowly. Generally speaking, the slower the better. This includes crayfish, Hellgrammite, and salamander imitations. The clearer the water and brighter the sunlight, the less you should move a fly that sits on the bottom. Learn to feel the light tick of a bass sucking it up off the grass, rocks, mud, or sand. When "swimming" a Hellgrammite,

Damsel Nymph, big Hex Nymph, or water snake imitation, use the figure eight retrieve to create consistent, smooth, slow motion of the fly. Other than the Grinnel Fly, I haven't caught many big bass on these types of flies, but it can happen in certain places at specific times in East Texas.

## *Safety First!*

I'm not going to reinvent the wheel, but I cannot write a book about fishing without talking about water safety. I was involved in a near-fatal boating accident when I was seven years old. I was already a well trained and strong swimmer who spent an average of ten hours per day in the water each Summer by that age. At twelve, I took both the Red Cross's Basic Rescue and Water Safety Course and their Advanced Lifesaving Course. I was not allowed to be certified as a Lifeguard until I was sixteen. I repeated that course and the Red Cross Water Safety Instructor course just before my sixteenth birthday. I worked the next three summers as a lifeguard, swimming and water safety instructor, and Waterfront Supervisor at a lake resort. At seventeen, I trained and tested an entire team of lifeguards and swift water rescue personnel, some of whom were twice my age. That training included small boat safety and rescue operations using rafts, canoes, and kayaks.

Later, in the military, I received a lot of small craft training from the U.S. Coast Guard and seamanship training from the U.S. Navy. Along the way, I've taken more courses in First Aid, CPR, and wilderness survival than I care to recount. I've also got a nationally recognized Boater Safety certification and am a member of the Adaptive Outdoor Safety Council. It's not that I'm obsessed with water safety. I simply never turned down an opportunity to receive authoritative training.

All I really want to say here is that in spite of all of that training, I wear a PFD religiously. In fact, it is because of all of that training that I wear a PFD religiously. I also carry a throw buoy with fifty feet of line with me in all boats. I always have at least one trauma kit handy. I carry extra rope, fasteners, reflective gear, lights, and tools with me almost everywhere I go.  A good sharp knife is as essential as socks and underwear.  I never get in a boat without a good knife capable of cutting nylon, Cordura, and even thin wire on my person.  A good pair of pliers is almost as essential.  And I honestly never head into the great outdoors without a top quality water filtration system and a high-volume whistle with me.

When it comes to water safety, the first line of defense is a properly sized Type I or Type II PFD for each person on a boat.  Even when hanging out on a dock or at a river, I have a throw line and buoy nearby.  I wade streams with quality footwear designed for that purpose and a staff.  You could be Michael Phelps and Jacques Cousteau rolled into one person and you can still drown in a few inches of water.  Lose consciousness or freedom of motion in the water and you are in trouble.  Most people have no appreciation for how badly adrenaline and cold water will debilitate a person until it is too late.  Water that is sixty degrees is almost forty degrees below your body temperature.  Your body will begin to lose core heat almost immediately after immersion. In an effort to keep your body warm, blood flow to the brain will be reduced. You'll get slow, groggy, euphoric, and then delirious. Next comes unconsciousness. Blood flow will also be reduced to your extremities as your body tries to preserve your internal organs. Your hands and feet will get heavy and awkward as your fine motor skills evaporate. This will happen with a minute or two to anyone who is not conditioned to the shock of sudden immersion in cold water – regardless of your fitness level. People who are extremely physically fit will be better able to combat these symptoms, but they will experience them. They will still succumb to them, perhaps a few minutes later than someone of typical fitness and athleticism. Combined with the adrenaline rush that accompanies any sudden life-threatening situation, you will have zero fine motor skills, quickly be out of breath, and you begin to become disoriented – headed toward unconsciousness. That PFD will save your life. You can still kick and move your arms in large, sweeping motions. You will tend to over-exert yourself due to the adrenaline rush. If you are held afloat by a PFD, you can probably get to safety – be it to the boat, the shore, or a substantial object that will allow you to keep your head above water long enough for someone to rescue you.

In moving water, the problems are compounded. Never under-estimate the invisible current in lakes and ponds we call "under-tow." Sub-surface currents can be quite strong. They are created mostly by the thermo-cline, or temperate differences, in the water. Shallow water heats up quickly in sunlight and cools quickly when the sun goes down, or anytime there is a major change in air temperature. Warmer water is lighter, and colder water is heavier. Cooler water in a shallow cove will sink below the warm surface layer and slide outward toward deeper water. This causes under-tow near shallow water. It will frequently be strong enough to sweep your feet out from under you. If you go below the surface and your entire body enters this sub-surface current, it can drag you out into deep water where you cannot stand up. Sometimes, it can be strong enough that pretty proficient swimmers...grown men...cannot break its pull and swim to the surface.

Trot-lines and fishing tackle can quickly ensnare someone's arms and legs in the water. So can aquatic plants. If this happens, you have whatever is left of your last breath of air to free yourself. Mud on the bottom can be a particularly ugly death trap. I've had to rescue people who tried to stand up, only to sink to their waist or beyond in sucking mud. This isn't easy and can quickly turn tragic.

Take a boater safety and/or water safety course. In fact, retake the course every few years just for grins and giggles. You can do it on-line for free in a couple of hours or less. Take the Red Cross or U.S. Coast Guard's basic rescue and water safety course. This course will give you minimal knowledge and skills required to safely and effectively help others in need of emergency assistance you may encounter on the water. These classes are cheap or free and usually take one or two days to complete.

Wear a good PFD.  I personally prefer high quality inflatable PFD's, because they are effective and comfortable to wear. Let's face it, if it isn't comfortable to wear a PFD you are less likely to wear it. *Having them in the boat does almost no good at all.*  While approved PFD's in the boat will keep you from getting a ticket, they will not save your life in an emergency. The data is overwhelming. *Wearing* a PFD is what saves lives. Yes, inflatable PFD's must be worn in order for them to make you legal, but *all* PFD's must be worn to save your life.  So I choose PFD's that are comfortable to wear and wear one at all times.  This keeps me legal, safe, and comfortable.

Keep a quality first aid kit close at hand at all times.  Follow all safety regulations for boating.  If you're supposed to have a serviceable fire extinguisher on board your boat, make sure you have a good one.  Don't settle for the minimum purchase that will get you past the game warden.  This goes for sounding devices and PFD's, too.  Just like that $20 I "saved" by not buying the net that cost me over a thousand dollar prize in the fishing tournament, you will never regret spending top dollar on quality safety equipment when you find yourself needing it. How much is it worth to have an incident that could ruin a family, much less a fishing trip, turn into just another adventure story about what happened yesterday at the lake? That's what good safety practices and equipment are worth. It's the difference between Jim fell out of the boat yesterday and died versus Jim fell out of the boat yesterday and we all had a good laugh at his expense. You choose. But everyone to whom it has happened also believed it would never happen to them.

If you want to have a long and fruitful adventure as a fisherman, you do what you can to protect that *long* part of the equation first and foremost. Because the more time you spend on the water, the more luck you'll experience and the more skill you'll develop; but you'll also be closer to that date with destiny when fortune favors the prepared.

## *In Closing*

There you have it. That's the extent of my fly-fishing for bass "bag of tricks." There's nothing really earth-shaking or unique in there. But I do know it all works better than the other stuff I've tried over the thirty-some-odd years I've been catching bass on a fly rod in East Texas. By no means do I think that I've got it down to a science, or that there isn't someone else out there doing something I haven't thought of or tried that works extremely well. I suspect that somewhere, someone is doing something I wish I were doing or using something I wish I knew about. I just haven't come across them yet.

I know of a hand full of fly-fishermen in Texas who have probably caught more really big bass than I have, but not many. I only know one man for sure who has caught one bigger on a fly rod, and perhaps three who have probably caught a few that were too close to argue about. I asked a few of those guys to contribute tips and techniques to this book, and they all told me "No, but thanks for asking." Guys who

John Lindsey with his 14 lbs. 4 ounce state fly rod record

Largemouth Bass, caught in 2000. (Image: Texas Parks and

Wildlife Department, 2000.)

consistently catch trophy fish tend to be fairly tight-lipped about how they do it unless you're paying them top dollar to teach you. The few really great fly-fishing guides in East Texas honestly don't need the extra publicity. They stay as busy as they want to be.

Me? I'm not a guide. I'm a teacher and an author. So what little money I do make from fishing comes mostly in the form of royalties from books and articles. Occasionally, I collect a speaker fee or something like that. Honestly, I used to be a duck hunting guide and I have a lot of friends who are fishing guides. Frankly, my disabilities make it unpredictable as to when I can fish hard and when I can't. So I don't guide. I prefer to fish a couple of days a week when I want to instead of having to fish four or five days a week when a client wants to. No thanks. Been there and done that with shotguns and dogs in the boat, in freezing water, the dark, and fog. But I do enjoy helping folks who want to learn and I enjoy writing. I hope you've enjoyed reading it half as much. And I hope there was at least one thing you gleaned from this book that helps you catch

bigger bass on the fly.

# *Epilogue*

*A Few Thoughts on Tournament Fishing*

Getting set up for the 2014 Bass on the Fly Championship on Lake Fork

The past several years have seen a new development in the tiny world of fly-fishing for bass:  the fly-fishing bass tournament.   In 2009, the first sanctioned fly-fishing tournament for Largemouth Bass was held on Lake Fork, *The Bass on the Fly Championship*, which just recently finished its fifth year. More fly-fishing bass tournaments are popping up here and there. The tournament fields are generally small, averaging about fifty boats each. I predict it won't be too long before we see our first one hundred boat field in a fly-fishing only bass tournament.

If you read this book, it may strike you that the tools, techniques, and overall strategy may require some modification for tournament fishing. You'd be correct. There is a distinct difference between choosing your fishery, times and dates, and techniques to optimize your chances of catching a trophy bass and fishing whenever, wherever the tournament organizers decide months in advance that the competition will take place. Furthermore, there is a difference in approach between methodically chasing that one truly exceptional bass with a fly rod and trying to make sure you post the biggest total length or weight of bass within a defined time-frame against other anglers.

Professional fishing guide, Carey Thorn, with one of his winning

bass from the Bass on the Fly World Championship tournament

on Lake Fork. (Image: Carey Thorn, 2013.)

Almost all tournament fishing is scheduled without regard to weather, seasonal changes in fishing patterns, and the fluctuation in boat traffic. Virtually all tournament fishing occurs from dawn until mid-afternoon, in order to accommodate the tabulation and posting of results and an awards ceremony before dark. Competitive anglers must be ready to fish in any conditions that are safe for small boat operations, and to adapt in such a way that maximizes their potential for catching an above average limit of the target species between sunrise and mid-afternoon. Almost all bass tournaments occur on weekends on popular lakes, so boating traffic will be at its peak for that time of year.

Most fly-fishing bass tournaments are planned on the Catch-Photo-Release format popularized by kayak fishing tournaments. The key is to score the fish with a photographic record, and is not just based on one's ability to catch them. Without wasting time or losing a fish overboard, you have to get the fish into the boat, get it laid out on a measuring tape, take a quality digital photograph, and release the fish unharmed. Then you've got to get right back to fishing.

One thing that you don't want to do in a fly-fishing tournament that is very common in conventional tackle bass tournaments is try to rush or "man-handle" your fish into the boat. Fly tackle cannot be good at presenting flies and good at muscling fish quickly to hand. Putting too much pressure on a fish while fly-fishing will almost always result in a lost fish. You still want to play the fish out by keeping moderate pressure on them, trying to coax them away from obstacles, and waiting for them to get winded. Then you land them carefully. This part simply cannot be rushed with a positive outcome with most fish species, because too much pressure will break your line, bend your hook, or tear the soft tissue that the hook penetrated. If you enlarge that hole in the soft tissue while fishing with barbless hooks, in particular, the chance of the fish throwing the hook goes up exponentially. But they will also come un-buttoned with barbed hooks far more often. I've been reading and hearing a lot about these so-called "specialty" fly rods for bass fishing lately, and how they're capable of "horsing" fish into the boat and out of cover. I've used them all pretty extensively. It's hype. Some rod designs can help wear a big fish down more quickly if you use the rod properly, but no fly rod is capable of "lifting" a fish. So this whole marketing gimmick about "lifting power" is very misleading.

Additionally, you must become very time-conscious when fishing competitively. You want to plan and prepare in advance to minimize the amount of time the other aspects of fishing take, to maximize the reliability of your equipment, and to avoid time-killing possibilities. This requires careful attention to everything from tow vehicles, boats, and trailers to lodging and meals, tackle, and other gear. For example, make sure your tow vehicle and trailer are in tip-top shape prior to a tournament weekend. Change the leaders on all lines that will be used and rig a separate rod and reel for each line you might fish. Clean and lubricate your reels as needed. Inspect the guides, grips, and reel seats on your rods.  Replace any flies that are worn or rusty.  Break out new spools of tippet.  Pack everything in a way that is easy to access and makes finding what you're looking for a breeze.  Labeling, clear water-tight containers, and organization skills become the small differences that can make the difference between winning and losing.  Make sure your maps are up to date and any electronics are operating at maximum capacity.  If you need something for trophy fly-fishing for bass, then you need *two of them* for tournament fly-fishing for bass.  Take at least one extra hat and one extra pair of quality sunglasses.  Never get caught with one "lucky fly" left in your fly box!  If you plan to fish a seven weight and a nine weight fly rod, take two seven weights and two nine weights.  Have all four rigged and ready to fish on your boat when you launch.

Remember that net I talked about in a previous chapter?  You need two nets if you can carry two safely on your boat.  Spare tires for truck and trailer are indispensible.  Make sure they're properly inflated.  First aid kits should be carefully planned to handle minor injuries quickly.  You can clean a wound later.  Stop the bleeding, dull the pain, immobilize the joint, cover that blister, and get back to fishing.  Think about medications for allergies, pain relief, indigestion, diarrhea, and a spray-on antiseptic.  Spend the two days prior to a tournament eating right and hydrating your body properly.  Carry plenty of water and some electrolytes on your boat.  You'd be amazed by how many amateur tournament anglers are knocked out of the running by dehydration, minor illnesses, and superficial injuries.  Hey!  If we're going to compete, let's *compete*!

Choose a boat that will comfortably and safely handle whatever conditions the fisheries you fish might throw at you.  This is more important than stealth when tournament fishing, because you cannot pick the weather.  If there is no Lake Wind Advisory or lightning at launch time, most tournaments will go on as planned.  You could be miles from the launch and have a major thunderstorm blow in with forty mile per hour winds, heavy rain, and lightning. The weather changes quickly in Texas! Many tournaments have a two-angler format per boat. You also want a boat that can cover "dead water" quickly without beating you to death between fishing spots. For all of these reasons, you'll likely choose a larger boat for tournament fishing than you otherwise would. These things are what drive the entire bass boat industry (in spite of the fact that only a small percentage of bass boat owners fish tournaments with any regularity).

This is like spitting into the wind, but I'll say it anyway. Don't drink alcohol the day (or night) before a tournament. Watch the caffeine, too. Caffeine and alcohol are diuretics, dehydrating your tissues at the cellular level. Same goes for nicotine. Cut back to minimal consumption. Muscle cramps are the first serious symptom of dehydration, and they'll knock you out of the saddle in a fishing tournament. Extra potassium can help stave off cramps. Eat a couple of bananas for breakfast.

If you're well prepared for competitive fishing, the part that happens on the water is far more manageable. Plan your fishing day(s) out in advance and stick to your plan. That means you need a fair weather and foul weather plan. Planning should include your selection of launch, fishing spots, and how to transit between them most efficiently. A good plan will include a minimum time per spot and a maximum time per spot without catching fish. You need to condense that timeline I gave in the last chapter by fifty percent, because now you have to run-and-gun until you find a group of four pound bass.

Basically, the target for a fly-fishing bass tournament is twenty inch Largemouth. If you can catch a limit of twenty inch Largemouth bass between sunrise and mid-afternoon, you will be in the final stretch to the podium. Your goal is to acquire that limit of twenty inch bass as quickly as possible. With time left, you can go to trying to catch bigger ones and culling the smallest ones first to pad your limit. You will replace any twenty inch fish with a twenty one inch fish. The difference between first and third place in most amateur catch-photo-release tournaments is less than two inches total length.

You'll want to eliminate your most time-consuming fishing tactics, so long as they are not your most dependable. Yeah, you may have landed your biggest bass by allowing a frog fly to sit motionless in the Lily Pads for a half hour. I get it. But you do not want to use that tactic in a tournament. Fish the tactics and flies that have landed you the most twenty inch/four pound bass. Period. You see, in a tournament, who catches that extra eight pound bass often determines the difference between first and second place. Sometimes, it's the difference between second and third. But they will usually all have a limit of twenty inch bass and one big fish. One thirty inch bass will lose a tournament to a limit of five twenty inch bass – one hundred inches beats thirty inches. There may be a prize for "biggest fish," and you may win it. But that isn't the "big money." The top honors are going to the angler who puts together the longest or heaviest total limit. Some tournaments run on a derby format, with hourly "weigh-in" and prizes for the biggest fish of the hour and variations on this theme. That would change almost everything about your strategy. So know the rules and design a strategy that maximizes your chance of success.

I've seen this happen many times in fishing tournaments. A guy catches his target limit (for example, that five fish limit of twenty inch bass) in the first forty-five minutes of competition. Then, thinking, "I've got this," he slacks off. Quite frequently, they will return to the weigh-in by mid-morning. They almost never win. Who wins? The angler who stayed out there and culled their smallest fish, replacing them with a half inch longer fish, is the person who wins. Quitters never win. Winners never quit. Of course, there is an exception to every rule. I've seen two guys out of hundreds quit by mid-morning and win a tournament, but they knew the fisheries well and recognized exceptional luck when they saw it in their boats. Both were professional guides fishing in amateur tournaments. They had lucked into limits within an hour of day break that they knew no one was likely to beat on any given day on those bodies of water. I still don't advise trying this if you actually care about winning.

Another thing that I have seen cost people money and prizes in fishing tournaments many times is not leaving themselves enough time at the end of the day to return to the "weigh-in" station and submit their results before closing time. In every case, they had calculated how long it would take and stopped fishing at that time. Then, some unforeseen circumstance (like a flat tire or fender bender in the parking lot or a motor that wouldn't start without some tinkering) cost them ten to twenty minutes. That extra ten to twenty minutes disqualified their "weigh-in." If you need thirty minutes to return to the weigh-in line from where you are fishing, you stop an hour before then. If you miss the close of the "weigh-in" line, you are disqualified. It does not matter what you caught. This is the most important thing to get right all day. What if everyone else is late and you caught one tiny fish?  You win, that's what!  And flat tires, fender benders, and motors that don't start are not "unforeseeable circumstances."  Who has not had that happen to them more often than they care to recall?  The challenge of tournament fishing is to foresee all the likely and possible scenarios and plan and prepare well for them.  That's how you win fishing tournaments – with just a bit of luck.

Fishing tournaments, I usually tie on slightly smaller flies than I do when hunting lunker bass just for fun.  I want flies that will catch me more four pound bass faster.  I'm not sure this makes much difference, because none of my flies are too big for a twenty inch bass to eat.  But it also helps me cast and fish with less fatigue and more accurately in windy conditions.  I'm not talking about going from a size 1 to a size 10 Wooly Bugger!  I'm talking about leaving that seven inch size 3/0 Deceiver in the box and fishing one that's five inches long and a size 1 hook instead.  Before a tournament, I'll spend time sharpening all of the hook points on my flies. Obviously, they don't *all* need it, but I check them all and touch up any that need it. I don't just clean my primary sunglasses. I clean the back-ups, too. Little things like this make the difference, and they turn a day of fun into a week of activity in anticipation. I'm no more obsessive than anyone else who has a real shot at winning any given tournament they may enter. The top tier players all play to win. I've been around several tournaments for several years in a row in both Florida and Texas, and I have observed that there is a core group of anglers who always seem to win the tournaments they enter. Maybe it will be any combination of three of the same nine guys or gals – over and over again. There are plenty more good anglers than that who enter the tournaments. If it were only luck, then there'd be a wider representation of individuals on the podiums. It's the best *competitors* among the good anglers who consistently win. If you're interested in competing in fly-fishing tournaments, learn to compete. Frankly, they're fun to fish and participate in even if you don't care about winning at all. You meet other fly anglers, fish some new water, and have a good time.  Nobody loses.  But it is a lot

more fun when you win!

www.ingramcontent.com/pod-product-compliance
Lightning Source LLC
Chambersburg PA
CBHW031946080426
42735CB00007B/289